Evaluating Press Coverage

Evaluating Press Coverage

A PRACTICAL GUIDE TO MEASUREMENT AND COST EFFECTIVENESS

David Phillips

KOGAN PAGE

First published in 1992

Apart from any fair dealing for the purposes of research or private study, or criticism or review, as permitted under the Copyright, Designs and Patents Act, 1988, this publication may only be reproduced, stored or transmitted, in any form or by any means, with the prior permission in writing of the publishers, or in the case of reprographic reproduction in accordance with the terms of licences issued by the Copyright Licensing Agency. Enquiries concerning reproduction outside those terms should be sent to the publishers at the undermentioned address:

Kogan Page Limited
120 Pentonville Road
London N1 9JN

© David Phillips, 1992

British Library Cataloguing in Publication Data
A CIP record for this book is available from the British Library
ISBN 0 7494 0530 9

Typeset by Books Unlimited (Nottm) – Sutton-in-Ashfield, Notts
Printed and bound in Great Britain by Biddles Ltd, Guildford and Kings Lynn

Contents

List of Figures 7
Acknowledgements 11

Introduction: How are You Doing in the Press? 13

1 Press Cuttings and the Press Cutting Bureaux 17
2 Measuring Coverage 28
3 Measuring Impact 41
4 Monitoring the Output 55
5 Press-Prompted Response 67
6 Attribution 78
7 The Competition as a Yardstick 101
8 Tracking Press Coverage 111
9 Press Targeting 127
10 Measurement Methodology 140
11 Monitoring as Advertising 143
12 Campaign Planning 149
13 Understanding Press Coverage for Effectiveness 159
14 International Press Programmes 169
15 Politics and Coverage 175
16 Corporate Coverage and Issue Management 181

17 The Effect on Public Relations Practitioners and the Media	189
18 Conclusions	198
Postscript	202

Appendices

1 Press Cutting Specification: a) Single Key Word b) Multi Key Word	206
2 Subcontractor/Consultancy Agreement	210
3 A Press Coverage Analysis	218
Index	233

List of Figures

2.1	The media and the market	29
2.2	Cutting bureaux response time	30
2.3	Articles published (to end of January 1991)	32
2.4	Press coverage (% of all column inches)	32
2.5	Measuring impact on the page	34
2.6a)	Cuttings received by week and month	
2.6b)	Cuttings received by week	37
2.7	Column centimetres published	38
2.8	Average articles per press release	38
2.9	Average article length (column centimetres)	39
2.10	Industry coverage – column centimetres of top 20 companies and others, 1990	39
3.1	Advertising and editorial perceived in different lights; significance of article size	43
3.2	Position on the page; key words in context; the importance of timing	45
3.3	Comparing editorial and advertising; headlines and photographs	46
3.4	Measuring column centimetres and area	49
3.5	Area comparisons for impact assessment	50
3.6	Ascribing values to measures of press articles	52

3.7	Methods for assessing message delivery effectiveness in core publications	53
4.1	Effective monitoring by Countrywide Communications	57
4.2	Typical analysis of 82 publications	60
4.3	Unsolicited articles published	62
4.4	Column centimetres per enquiry	62
4.5	How enquiries follow share of coverage	63
4.6	Enquiries as a result of editorial coverage	64
5.1	Style and content can provoke tremendous response	74
6.1	Issues tracking from coast to coast: CARMA gallops ahead . . .	88
6.2	Attitudes in the USA to the European Single Market: leading favourable/unfavourable arguments	88
6.3	Leading coverage by country (% of total: 1989 vs 1990)	89
6.4	Leading sectoral issues (% of total: 1989 vs 1990)	90
6.5	Leading sources of news: 1989	91
6.6	Leading sources of news: January-March 1990	91
7.1	Industry coverage in ccm of top 20/client/others	101
7.2	Press coverage in 1990: selected releases/product appearances	105
7.3	Industry coverage in ccm in selected journals 1990	106
7.4	Industry coverage: appearances in selected journals 1990	106
7.5	Industry coverage: appearances of top 20 companies and others 1990	108
7.6	Average articles per press release	109
8.1	Press releases issued to the end of January 1991	112
8.2	Articles published to the end of January 1991	112
8.3	Column centimetres published to the end of January 1991	113

List of Figures

8.4	Client A: ccms published over a three-year period	114
8.5	Company B: ccm per article	114
8.6	Client A: cuttings for client and competition	117
8.7	Total client industry coverage (ccm) over four months	118
8.8	Total client industry coverage (ccm) over twelve months	121
8.9	Journals covering client industry over two years	124
9.1	Reach of coverage spreadsheet	129
9.2	Opportunities to read (circulation)	130
9.3	Typical record of a journal covering a client	133
9.4	Matching geographic areas and target audiences to identify potential message delivery	137
10.1	Penetration in available articles – Boss Trucks Limited	142

Acknowledgements

In the preparation of this book I have been greatly helped by many in the public relations business both in the UK and in the USA. Particular thanks to Jon White for keeping my feet on the ground and Sandra Macleod and others for their enthusiastic support. To Keith Wootton I reserve most thanks for having to intellectualise and follow through much of the logic as well as prepare many of the charts, and finally Margaret Mayell and Pat Benton for turning this text into English.

Introduction: How are You Doing in The Press?

As this book goes to press, services to measure the effectiveness of press relations have mushroomed. Some consultants have used press relations measurement as their own unique selling proposition for a number of years. Now measuring press coverage has become a much more widespread and important part of press relations. It is long overdue, as is a book which covers the topic.

Countless managers who spend money on public relations still do not know who is good at press relations and have no yardstick to assess excellence. There is wholesale uncertainty over how to assess value and ensure cost effectiveness and, with no recognised means of assessing competence, expectations are low.

Where is the quantifiable benefit? Budgets are low because skilled measurement of PR is rare. With the advent of the new press coverage analysis services it is time to review what is practical and cost effective. Certainly, the importance of detailed analysis, available for a few hundred pounds, deserves some investigation. What these services might offer also needs to be explored.

Until recently, Institute of Public Relations (IPR) members were barred, under their code of conduct, from providing performance-related press relations. Although many consultants have measurement systems, there were few incentives, and every excuse, to avoid professional measurement with bite. Under the new IPR rules the Institute will have to look again at the question of guaranteed coverage being an incentive for payment. It is hoped that this book, and the consultants already measuring press relations and offering it as a service, will soon lead the competition to discover who can

Evaluating Press Coverage

realistically out-bid whom for measurable effect. Measuring press relations effectiveness will be part of the equation.

For the future, excellence will be measured.

The best practitioners will not only outshine less competent kin, they will be able to demonstrate by how much. Consultants want a unique selling proposition and will use many methods to show how unique their services are. People who buy press relations will be able to let their expectations soar.

Working with clients who believe in press and public relations can provide an opportunity to rise above the average, research and publish the result. With constant evaluation and comparative analysis, press and public relations can be planned to be very cost effective. Known, predictable, measured effectiveness is both possible and essential for proper press relations management. Here, at least, is a bench-mark upon which others can add their criticisms and perfection.

It is important to note the difference between measuring effectiveness in obtaining coverage and the impact of press relations in influencing attitudes. In its broader definition there is no single guide to measuring public relations effectiveness and although press work is a small part of developing beneficial relationships, it is also a very important element in the wider role for planned PR. A survey of Institute of Public Relations members, carried out by the Cranfield School of Management in July 1991, found that 68 per cent regarded the media as their main public and that 87 per cent regarded media pressure as an important issue in their work.

Once your media achievements are assessed, you are in a better position to discover your wider public relations needs. Evaluation of coverage is the first step towards effective planning and allocation of resources. Intelligence gleaned from adding an elementary statistical measure to the chore of reading press cuttings shows how effective you and your competitors are. The difference between counting cuttings and their content, which is not much of a measure, and applying rules to find out if the cuttings are of value is an important one.

Media coverage has an impact on the attitudes of people, but its quantifiable effectiveness as an opinion former is a much more elusive animal. The academic view, based on studies of, for example, the effects of violence on TV, is that the media reinforces existing opinions or behaviours, while diffusion of innovation research suggests that the media serves to bring information to public

Introduction: How are You Doing in the Press?

attention and that action is stimulated by other influences. These theories will be examined in light of recent content analysis surveys to see how powerful media impact really can be. The potency of the media, which depends on (often stretched) public credulity, is shifting sand in itself, but it is unquestionably powerful. With a reliable and constant form of appraisal the role and value of public relations can be more closely aligned with the effectiveness of the media.

What follows is a guide for those organisations requiring measured performance and effective management for their press relations activities.

Most of the profession has spent more than a little time trying to find a quantitative and qualitative measure for press relations work. By 1990, seven or more of the major consultancies had spent a great deal of time trying to come up with a generally useable model, some of which are very sophisticated. There is even a consensus and generally accepted approach. (Hitherto, the real problem has been a desire to establish how attitudes and behaviour are affected through the media. An Olympian ambition indeed and, until some generally accepted rules are applied, this advanced stage is too far from achievement for mere mortals in the public relations business.) Execution, however, is another matter. In general, if only for good internal management, statistical measurement should be simple, cheap and easy to administer.

First, what can be measured easily should be established. If it then contributes to the campaign, use it. If not, don't.

For the most part, current levels of sophistication are not yet competent in comprehensively tracking changing attitudes. While mass opinion forming is more often affected by a narrow band of media such as TV, radio and national newspapers, the level of general experience and detailed, academic research using broad-based, commonly accepted measures has not yet validated the work of the high-flyers in this field. Managers need to understand and believe the predictive qualities of numerate press cuttings evaluation. They also need to see the tangible benefits of carrying this out. Right now they remain suspicious and need more exposure to what is practical.

Companies and concerns which do not follow advances in the field had better wake up. By 1990 it was possible to say with absolute knowledge and conviction how much, what type, where and, to a large extent, when press coverage was needed for a company as it

Evaluating Press Coverage

moved from fourth to first place market share. Attitudinal change could also, in a less sophisticated way, be identified and tracked using media coverage as the means.

Offering such facilities to every manager at an acceptable cost is gradually becoming possible. All that is required is to insist upon its use to avoid wasting any more of those press relations budgets.

What horizons measurement can open up! Imagine for a moment knowing what attitudinal changes the media will accomplish between dinner and breakfast time and being able to pre-empt them. What price knowing how to achieve such an attitudinal change? In the not too distant future some of this will be possible. For now we must be content to put down some simple ground rules on the way to find out what we can measure, and thereby plan and set targets.

Realistically, this book is about most press relations programmes for more ordinary-sized budgets. That is not to say it is irrelevant to large companies. The greatest benefits will be derived by organisations such as companies with a number of operating subsidiaries.

1

Press Cuttings and the Press Cutting Bureaux

Much of our history is held on baked clay, ageing skins, parchment and paper; a source of great joy to humanist and historian alike. For as long as most of us can remember, press clippings have been eminently collectable; we all recall the many cinema depictions of actors waiting up for first night reviews and ageing actresses poring over notices of past glories. But for people and organisations whose livelihoods depend on fame, more recent cuttings have an immediate importance.

There have always been the propagandists whose function was to persuade the journalist to write about people and activities and thereby improve the volume and, possibly, quality of such coverage. In all the best movies, press relations skill was always measured by the fatness of clippings books and woe betide the press agent if the newspapers panned the play.

Political, corporate and personal fame and fortune is often made through the media and the skilled press officer still turns to the trophy book to prove his worth and obtain more work. Others might deride this trophy book as being only a small part of the work they do and there is a feeling that the person who asks to see it is somehow only looking at past glory. To some extent this is true, but let us not forget that reading press clippings is still the most important measure of fame, if not fortune.

Professional pride, a bad report or a press campaign going off course are critical to confidence while the feel and sense of media reaction is of vital importance.

Reading and getting a human feel for cuttings, what they represent and their interpretation still requires the personal touch.

While it may be supported by much analysis, there is no substitute for a good read. This then is the most important part of measuring press relations effectiveness.

Before venturing too far into the mechanisms for monitoring, measuring and evaluating press coverage, a process universally called 'content analysis', it is worth a quick review of some of the background.

Content analysis

The study of the writing of individuals and collected published and private contributions of a wide range of authors, has long been an activity for historians and social scientists. By studying scripts, the tale they tell and the influences at work on the author and publisher, a great deal can be learned. In the 1930s social scientists began to use content analysis in the USA and the technique gained practical significance during the Second World War when various branches of the American Government sponsored systematic reviews and analyses of the Nazi press for intelligence purposes. Thus began this means of taking messages that are conveyed as a part of the communications process, coding and classifying them as precisely and objectively as possible, and then summarising and explaining them quantitively.

This process has a number of very valuable attributes:

- it can provide an overview of the communication of ideas, concepts and the accepted mores of the day;
- it allows us to track major political, social and economic trends, the progress of technology and impact of individual institutions;
- it can also help us measure overall effect of publicly distributed messages.

For 30 years after the war the use of content analysis developed little as opinion polls seemed to be more efficient and economical. But in the early 1980s renewed interest came about as researchers wanted to find out more about what people were doing, rather than what they were saying, and the influences which were at work on them.

Researchers found that content analysis can measure actual media behaviour as opposed to focusing on how those who work for the media feel about something. In the USA Maxwell E Combes, David

H Weaver, Donald L Shaw, Jack Mcloed and Robert D Mclure have been leading academics in this area and gave content analysis considerable momentum in the 1980s. Walter Lindenmann (Ketchum Public Relations), A J Barr (CARMA International) and John E Merriam (Conference on Issues and Media) have become leading exponents in the USA with transplants into the UK. Companies such as AT&T, Rothmans and Ingersoll Rand as well as the European Commission have experience of and use evaluation services to monitor and evaluate media coverage. Many others now actively use these techniques and the trend is growing.

One of the most famous examples of content analysis is the best selling book by John Naisbitt, *Megatrends: Ten New Directions Transforming Our Lives* (1982, Warner Books Inc, New York). He identified trends using content analysis of many thousands of articles relating to local news events in 125 daily newspapers in the USA.

As we can now watch how the media is setting trends, it is worth examining how it is done.

Getting the cuttings

At first glance, it may seem relatively easy to specify press cuttings but, as the need to be more sophisticated and the number of publications grows, specifying precisely what is required becomes more demanding. There is no doubt that much of the disappointment expressed over cuttings is a result of poor specification and lack of problem diagnosis.

In this information era, sourcing every cutting about anyone or anything is an awe inspiring task. In Britain alone, over twenty thousand regularly published journals cover all manner of news and views. Even the actress waiting for first night reviews has an immense task in buying all the relevant publications. She will have to wait for weekly and monthly periodicals and then seek to find out what the syndicated coverage might be. Armed with the most likely newspapers from the corner shop, the tension rises as each page is turned. A rave review in the dailies but what will the weeklies say?

For the corporate manager with a city audience the problem can be even worse. The profusion of newspaper coverage added to radio, television and electronic media is mind boggling. The media has a dramatic impact on the corporate manager's daily life. He too has to watch what the trade papers say and how correspondents reflect the corporate story.

Media coverage is global. News follows both the sun and money. From Wall Street to Tokyo, on to Hong Kong and then to the London Stock Exchange, electronic media works round the clock, supplying leads to journalists in the evening for morning editions next day.

Sourcing the news means constant worldwide tracking. This fast-flowing stream is swelled by the immense weight of additional information aimed not only at journalists and commentators but at people who make day-to-day decisions based on what they read. Direct mail, on-line databases and one-on-one letters and memos are a few such examples.

However, this book concerns the press, and we will concentrate in this area where the level of expertise is frequently very high and impact quite extraordinary. Specialist journalism on daily, weekly and monthly periodicals is exceptional in volume and, usually, quality and a happy hunting ground for those who specialise in providing background briefing material and press releases which shape the journalists' point of view.

The press cutting bureaux

For most of us, the news stand as the principal source for press clippings is far too unreliable and we cannot spend sufficient time going through all that newsprint. We go instead to one of the many press cutting bureaux. Typical reading lists are huge, with specialists covering different areas and the leading bureaux incorporating sections dedicated to specific types of publication such as:

- trade and specialist;
- foreign press;
- national daily;
- consumer, etc.

Certain specialist organisations, however, operate selectively. Some, such as the electronic reports provided by FT Profile in the UK, are massive databases accessible 'on-line' . Using a simple computer and modem, copy from newspapers and business magazines is available to everyone within hours of publication. These computer-based agencies tend to cover a limited number of journals.

Among the press cutting bureaux, real expertise can be found. With such large numbers of journals, a bureau's training and systems will concentrate on picking up every single mention of the client, actress, product or event. The best in the field are staggeringly good. Of course, they miss the occasional mention, and there are no rebates for such misses, but compared to their success rate, failure is minuscule. Here is the pinnacle of reading for key words and selected subjects.

However, for some of the evaluation measures we discuss in this book, even this service has its drawbacks: a lot of the impact and sense of what is said in the press comes from where the mention appears in the publication and its position on the page. Nevertheless, this information can be isolated with close co-operation with the bureau concerned.

Selecting a bureau

There is every good reason to be careful in selecting a bureau, and some understanding of how it operates is invaluable. The essence of measuring press relations starts with this source of information but there are important limiting factors:

- *Coverage* can be determined only for publications received by the bureau and is limited by the resources available to read them.

- *Accuracy* depends on the performance of individual readers. The bureau of your choice will need to have an extensive training organisation to be effective but even the best readers sometimes miss cuttings. References to regular or known customers and subjects are rarely overlooked. Cuttings are more likely to be missed for short-term orders or customers with a low score rate than for any other reason.

- *Delay* can occur as journals are published at different intervals, publishing dates change and cuttings may not come in chronological order. It is not uncommon for publishers, for a variety of mostly understandable reasons, to forget or delay sending copies to the cutting bureaux. The weekly free sheets are among the worst offenders.

Evaluating Press Coverage

Of course, a press cutting bureau will want to know precisely what it is looking for. Before even considering the bureau, a clear set of objectives is essential.

Setting objectives

1 To find all the relevant cuttings (dealt with below) within an acceptable timescale Who does not like (under most circumstances) to see his or her name in print? Every cutting has its own value and what may seem obscure to one may be very significant to another. There are occasions when cuttings will be sought only where they mention one key word, company, organisation, product or issue. On other occasions competitors or whole industries are important and relevant.

2 To evaluate importance and content Once we have the cutting it is always important that it is read by someone who can evaluate the importance and content of what is written. Many cuttings provide extra information which can be used for a variety of purposes. There may be an opportunity for a salesman, a designer or financial manager; some cuttings provide vital competitor information or raise issues not yet properly considered by the organisation. This is why a designated person should always read all clippings for the information provided.

3 To assess the relevance and reach (circulation or readership) of the journal Most cuttings confirm information, such as the relevance of the publication, and can be used to establish core publications and important niche journals where an audience is important but may have been overlooked. Bear in mind that some publications may have a small but very important circulation. Cuttings often provide news of a hitherto unknown publication, which will need to be checked out for its importance or relevance.

4 To evaluate press relations activity For many, the cutting will be the result of considerable hard work, so we look at cuttings for the effectiveness of our own or others' press relations activity.

These objectives will be supplemented by others according to your own requirements and will need to be listed before specifications can be properly put to your cutting bureau.

Press cutting bureaux are as good as the brief they are given. Most look to the customer to provide a key word or series of key words to assist them in their selection.

Key words

A person or subject is identified throughout the media by a word or words which are as specific to the person or subject as can be, if not unique. These are known as 'key words'. Frequently this is a company, product or brand name. Using this principle, the bureau can identify subject matter and clip the relevant article. It will also cut for a key word appearing in a photograph caption and in advertisements.

Identifying a unique key word can be quite demanding. The actress analogy shows how difficult key word identification can be: there are enough children named after actresses and actors to confuse the issue for all time and for years after a block busting musical. Take a product called Hoover. To specify the word Hoover, which is used as a generic for all manner of vacuum cleaners, could mean a pile of cuttings of little relevance to the product's promotion. In this instance, the objective and brief may need to be very precise. The key word may be for the product alone but the objective may be much wider. It is possible that Hoover will want to know about all references to vacuum cleaners. It may want to know what competitors are up to or, indeed, may like to see where there are instances of 'passing off'. While the brand or generic term 'Hoover' will certainly lead to most cuttings, the phrase 'vacuum cleaner' will identify even more. However, to be sure of catching every relevant cutting, it may be necessary to specify some more phrases, such as 'industrial cleaner' or 'suction sweeper', especially if competitors are trying to position their products with different names.

Fortunately, the good cuttings bureaux are all too familiar with this. Romeike and Curtice is one of the largest bureaux in the UK and is well aware of the limiting factors. The bureau has kindly prepared notes for this book which are reproduced in their entirety:

What the bureau looks for

The bureau will look for a brief which is clear and unambiguous. To be successful you will need to observe the following rules:

1. Make clear exactly what key words are required. This is the most important aspect since the readers will work from these and will send cuttings only from articles in which they occur.
   (a) One should make sure that the key words supplied are those that will appear. For example, if an association appears regularly under its acronym and not in full, unless the acronym is a key word the mention will not be sent.
   (b) One should make sure that, if necessary, there is a brief explanation of what the company does or what the product is, and so on. There are many examples where two or three products have the same name.
   Each bureau will rewrite the brief to suit its own house style and should confirm the instructions. If in doubt as to whether the brief has been correctly interpreted, call the bureau to clarify the issue.
2. Be precise about what you want to be cut. Do you want every single reference or do you want only product mentions? There are many different restrictions that can be placed.
3. From what media do you want cuttings? If you are sending press releases to regional weeklies, do you want cuttings from the trade and technical press as well? Does the bureau read the publications you are interested in? Ask for a reading list.
4. How frequently do you require cuttings? Most bureaux despatch twice a week, although some may despatch daily. If you require cuttings very quickly, do you need a fast service which delivers cuttings from the national press by 8 am?

To help the bureau:

Low yield: Tell the bureau if something has appeared, do not wait to see if it is picked up. The best bureaux know they should pick it up, but if they do not, others may be missed too and readers can be given a special alert to make sure all coverage is cut.

Briefing considerations to discuss with the bureau

Before visiting the bureau you will need a comprehensive brief. To help work out what you need to have with you, the following items may need to be considered.

Press Cuttings and the Press Cutting Bureaux

Are the cuttings to include mentions about:

- an issue?
- a company or an organisation?
- an industry or clearly defined interest?
- products or services?
- product or service generic?
- acronyms and abbreviations?

Type of cutting to include:

- all references or product mentions only;
- full page when appearance occurs.

Distinguish between:

- those for regular delivery;
- fast delivery;
- those for rush delivery (usually before 8 am).

To include with the cutting:

- reason for cutting;
- when and where references in the press occur.

Reasons for cutting:

- to identify opportunities for the organisation;
- to identify competitors and competitor activity;
- to stay abreast with industry, or special interest issues;
- to identify reach (circulation)
- to monitor publications with an interest;
- to assess impact;
- to quantify effectiveness of press relations;
- to identify important writers and commentators.

Anticipated publications:

- predominantly national, regional, special interest, business, trade and technical, other;
- typical publication sample;
- frequency;
- exclusions if any;
- typical audiences/readers;
- position, interest in reading, what information is sought (news, background, technique, data).

Coverage:

- all references, product only, exclusions

Useful additional information:

- name and activity of the organisation or company;
- person who will be responsible for cuttings and the principal reader.

Monitor effectiveness and follow up

Once you are in receipt of cuttings, you can assist your bureau to maintain its effectiveness by following a number of simple rules:

Keep a management log The first step is to keep a simple log of cuttings as they arrive. This will be a list giving each cutting a reference number, journal name, publication date, receipt date and (if possible) the number of days taken for the cutting to arrive.

A cutting record showing the minimum, maximum and average number of days taken to arrive this month, which can be compared month on month, will be useful. A note of whether the clipping is from a monthly, weekly or daily publication is important. It is also important to know which cuttings are not relevant. You should be looking for a continuous improvement for each of these measures as mutual experience is gained.

Maintain circulation lists As circulation lists are generated, be aware of your changing media targets and keep the bureau informed. From time to time send copies of lists to the bureau to help it keep reading lists up to date.

Note unusual mentions Keep the bureau informed of any anticipated individual mentions, or if something is likely to appear out of context.

Return any incorrect cuttings Not only is the cost credited but, more important, it shows the reader what the client needs. It may contribute to a change in instructions, reducing the chances of future mistakes.

Check cuttings Make sure the cuttings you receive reflect your requirements.

Visit the bureau Knowing how the bureau works, and the people involved, is of vital importance. Keeping in touch with your account executive at the bureau will ensure you get the best out of the cutting service. This is good communications and management practice and is appreciated by your bureau.

Press cutting specification

In ensuring that a comprehensive brief is given to a bureau, it is important not to miss the essentials and the guide given in Appendix 1 may be of value to you. Most bureaux have their own application forms which include some of the detail given in this guide. You may consider supplementing their form with a more detailed description.

With this detailed briefing we are now in a better position both to receive and expect to receive all the press clippings we need and to miss very few.

2

Measuring Coverage

Press coverage analysis requires a very different attitude to cuttings. It is common practice to view each cutting on its own merits and, while there is every good reason to do so, we are moving on from there to a point where we view coverage in the round. We are now looking not at what one publication may say but at a much broader view. Our interest is now what 'the press' is saying. We view the media in its totality, not as a series of publications but its effect and influence throughout its complexity and diversity.

Being able to analyse coverage from this wider standpoint can produce some interesting results.

Issues and trends

To understand why we should want to move on to more complex measures it is worth pausing to look at some of the interesting tracking work which is more common in the USA.

John E Merriam, chairman and president of the Conference on Issues and Media in Alexandria, Washington reported in *American Demographics* (February, 1991), that the National Media Index built up trend lines which tracked how media exposure can mould public response. Coverage on environmental issues in the USA between 1984 and 1988 foreshadowed rising public demand for spending on environmental protection and dramatic growth in sales of organic foods (Figure 2.1). Interestingly, Merriam found that specialist media offered the earliest clues and concluded: 'If you want to know who's winning the computer wars, it makes sense to measure the exposure of different brands in popular computer magazines before you look in general circulation newspapers.'

Measuring Coverage

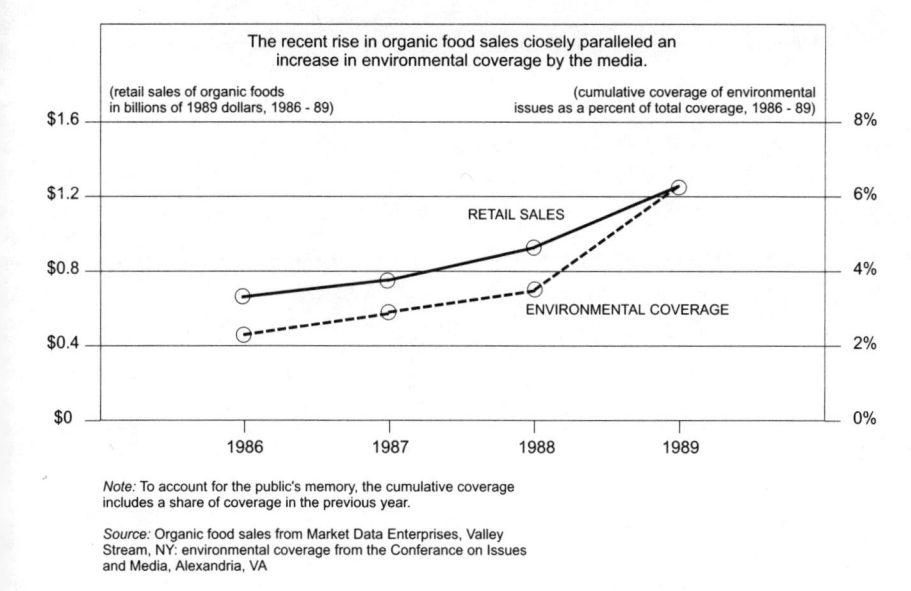

Figure 2.1 The media and the market

Chart title: The recent rise in organic food sales closely paralleled an increase in environmental coverage by the media.

Left axis (retail sales of organic foods in billions of 1989 dollars, 1986 - 89): $0 to $1.6
Right axis (cumulative coverage of environmental issues as a percent of total coverage, 1986 - 89): 0% to 8%
X-axis: 1986, 1987, 1988, 1989

Series shown: RETAIL SALES, ENVIRONMENTAL COVERAGE

Note: To account for the public's memory, the cumulative coverage includes a share of coverage in the previous year.

Source: Organic food sales from Market Data Enterprises, Valley Stream, NY: environmental coverage from the Conferance on Issues and Media, Alexandria, VA

Effectiveness of press offices

There is another reason for tracking coverage in a wider context. We can measure the effectiveness of press relations campaigns and thereby put a real value on the services offered both in-house and by consultants who organise such activities.

Our interest in measuring the wider press is now much more absorbing than a simple guard book and can be very useful in many ways. Such comprehensive understanding begins with basic systems and disciplines.

Once a reliable source for press cuttings has been found, the first simple measurements can begin.

Measuring the press cuttings

Know how many cuttings are received

Keeping a regular record of how many cuttings have arrived is essential. A tally of receipt dates ensures that the agency is keeping the flow of news up to date and can help monitor coverage month by month. A simple monthly record could look like Figure 2.2.

Evaluating Press Coverage

Cutting reference	Publish date	Date received	Days to arrive
1 D	1.3.91	6.3.91	5
2 W	4.3.91	6.3.91	2
3 M	3.91	6.3.91	–
4 W	11.1.91	6.3.91	50
5			
6			
7			
etc.			

Average: 14.25 ($^{57}/_4$)

Maximum days this month   50
Minimum days this month   Nil
Average days this month   14.25
Average days last month   6.1

D = daily
W = weekly
M = monthly

Figure 2.2 Cutting bureaux response time

Keep cuttings in a chronological order

The number of cuttings being regularly received is the basis for knowing what to expect each week, month or year. Fluctuations in output of press releases and press briefings can be detected and trends in press coverage will become noticeable. Filing and analysing cuttings, even at the simplest level, needs careful thought to avoid needless time-wasting and expense.

Most public relations activity is maintained on a monthly cycle between reporting meetings (although there may well be numerous meetings and contact in the interim). In these circumstances it will be worth measuring coverage to coincide with the reporting meeting. In other cases it may be important to provide reports at more frequent intervals and press coverage measurement may need to be reviewed each time.

How to keep cuttings is always something of a problem. Cuttings do not arrive chronologically. The reasons include: differing monthly publication dates, the speed at which the cutting bureau works and even the vagaries of the postal system. Archiving cuttings in strict date order is therefore a problem unless we are prepared to wait up to six weeks or more before filing. Most people need to see coverage as it is identified and will be prepared for some cuttings to be included in a later month. So there are alternative methods available.

Get the cuttings read

Reference to archiving as the next process after receipt of cuttings is because this is all too often the case. Of course it is vital that cuttings should be read, but many managers who regularly receive a lot of cuttings from the press office have little time to read them all. To avoid cuttings being discarded (or archived) unread, a short report about the coverage and a system for identifying important trends is frequently valuable.

As we have seen from the previous chapter, it is important to check that cuttings are germane and relevant as soon as they arrive in order to ensure that the cutting bureau's brief and clipping are accurate and effective. One of the first sets of measurements will be to distinguish coverage for the client from that for competitors and pinpoint those articles which cover both types.

Checklist for press cutting

- *Reporting interval*: Will it be daily/weekly/monthly?
- *Archive*: Will cuttings be archived as they arrive or in date published order (or both)?
- Are cuttings recorded as they arrive?
- Do cuttings refer only to the client?
- Are cuttings shared by client and competition?
- Do cuttings refer only to competitors?

Illustrative methods

With this information a very revealing picture of the coverage received can be generated. A simple bar chart such as that in Figure 2.3 demonstrates coverage for a company. Over a period of time, a comprehensive view emerges.

Evaluating Press Coverage

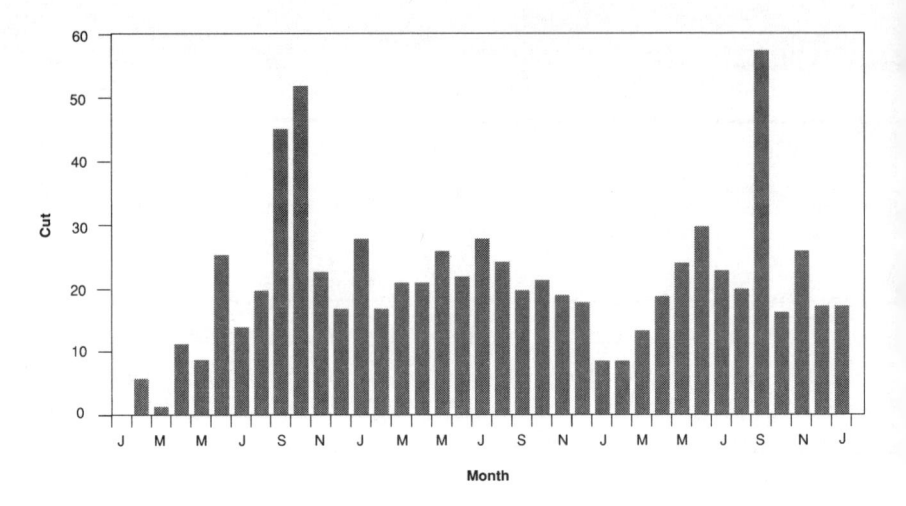

Figure 2.3 Articles published (to the end of January 1991)

Clearly (in Figure 2.3) we can see a cyclical downturn in the last three months of the year, together with the impact of certain events – in this case a corporate identity change and product launches. On this bar chart, cuttings are entered for the month they are published and not for the date they were received.

Composite charts can also be kept as shown in Figure 2.4

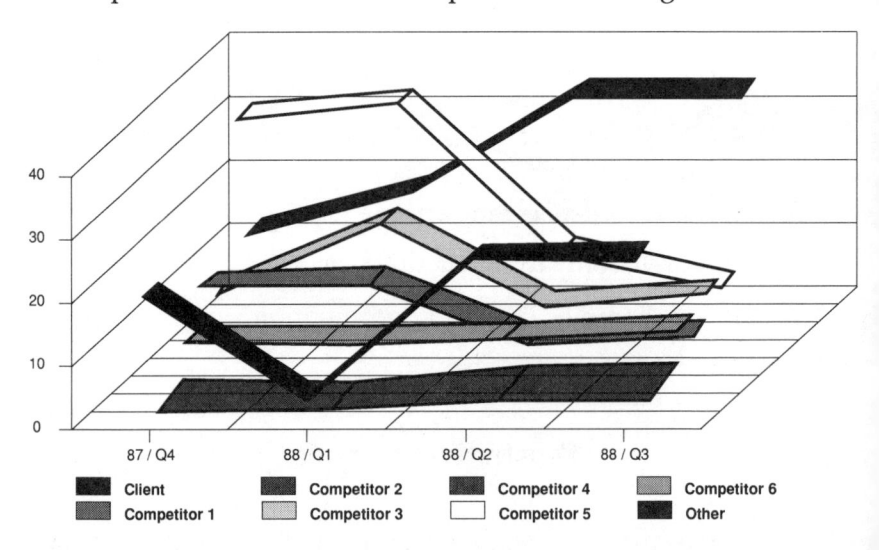

Figure 2.4 Press coverage (% of all column inches)

A chart kept like this will show a comparison between client and competitors and will also show when competitors are active and if they are changing the resource behind press coverage. A refinement for this kind of measurement is to separate out a particular product range or subject area. For example, simple filtering for a client would allow measurement of the number of cuttings about corporate, local and product news.

We have seen that keeping a record about coverage provides considerable information about the nature of press mentions in a particular industry and for a company and its competitors. So far we have looked at the number of articles which can be attributed to a client and its competitors. Progressively we can look in more depth.

Identifying coverage on the page

There are long articles and short articles, ones with photographs and those with banner headlines. This kind of measurement begins to help us identify the impact of editorial, but a method for measuring impact is required.

Word counts

To count the number of words in an article is undoubtably a tedious occupation, as Figure 2.5 illustrates. Even using computer scanners, word counts have limitations. There are bureaux specialising in this field which will also be able to add total circulation and a breakdown of the relevant readership.

However, for most analysis such detail is unnecessary and other measures will be required to find out what impact has been achieved. For example, counting words will not give an indication of the sheer size on the page. Measurement of the space taken by a photograph will also be needed to give an impression of the coverage. Experience and several spot checks over some 20,000 column centimetres (ccm) of newsprint and 1000 cuttings for one client alone shows that the effect on evaluation of counting words or an alternative measurement of column centimetres has little effect on the usable data. Manipulation of the statistics of word count collected requires a lot of processing before any meaningful information is forthcoming.

Evaluating Press Coverage

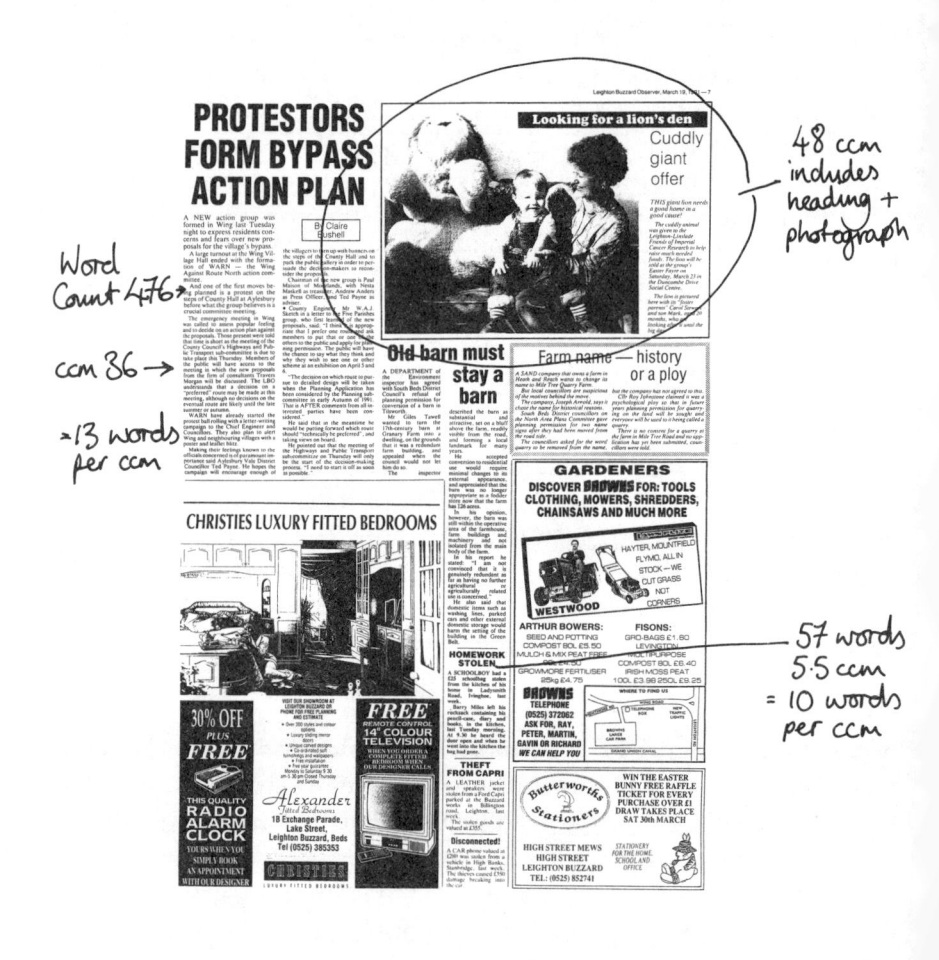

Figure 2.5 Measuring impact on the page

34

Unless the measurement is to find out if coverage has the same effect as for advertising, word count has few uses.

Measure space

There are other evaluations which can be considered. For example the width of a column as an impact measure, position *on* the page and position *of* the page are more sophisticated features.

The important part of this exercise was (and remains) not to change the method mid-evaluation. In the UK, where electronic storage of published material is not very comprehensive (with only a few organisations such as FT Profile providing a service), counting centimetres is easier, quicker and cheaper. It can take into account the presence and influence of photographs and the impact off the page of a big headline. What it does not do is measure column width.

In time, comprehensive databases may cover more than national dailies and a few business journals, which will make a substantial difference to the way we measure. Meanwhile, we must seek a usable and simple means of effective assessment.

Column centimetres is such a measure.

Column centimetres

How one justifies the difference between measuring effectiveness in column centimetres in the *Sun* and *Wall Street Journal* is superficially difficult. In reality the difference is not so much the actual size but the readership and content. Relatively minor sophistication in a good measurement system will iron out such difficulties. But, without more academic research, quantifying such differences for useful analysis is not yet available for the majority of PR practitioners.

For the purist, the difference between column centimetres (ccm) and word count was found to be less than 5 per cent per 1000 cuttings over 15,000 words across random coverage for an industrial company. Here the research was based on the impact of coverage across the target readership and bore content in mind. In this small sample, data such as total readership and analysis of readership showed that the difference in readership was much more important than columnar spread. The varied messages in the coverage achieved reflected different levels of acceptance between readerships.

The net effect was that column centimetres columnar spread made only a small difference in impact.

When counting column centimetres there needs to be a set of rules which will always apply. Changing the rules at any stage will distort the findings.

'Key word' mentions

Depending on how evaluation is to be achieved, several systems are available, but for most coverage there will be two important measures:

1. A count of the number of mentions of a key word
2. A 'nominal' length of coverage given to the appearance of a key word which can be directly attributed to it.

In most cases a key word will be a product, brand or company and, in the 'nominal' length type of measure, one column centimetre can be attributed to the appearance of the key word.

Include photographs

Column centimetres can be counted as:

- a total of all the column centimetres from the top of the headline to the end of the last column to the nearest ccm rounded down including photographs (see Figure 2.5 on page 34);
- as above but excluding headline;
- as above but excluding photograph.

As most coverage measurement is aimed at measuring impact values, the most frequently used measure is the total figure from top to bottom of an article inclusive of headline and photograph. The effect of measuring the size of an article in total is an important measure when applied to a relevant yardstick.

Reporting frequency

Making reports about different types of measurement has to be considered against the coverage that is to be measured. If cuttings are to be principally sources from monthly journals, reporting at

Measuring Coverage

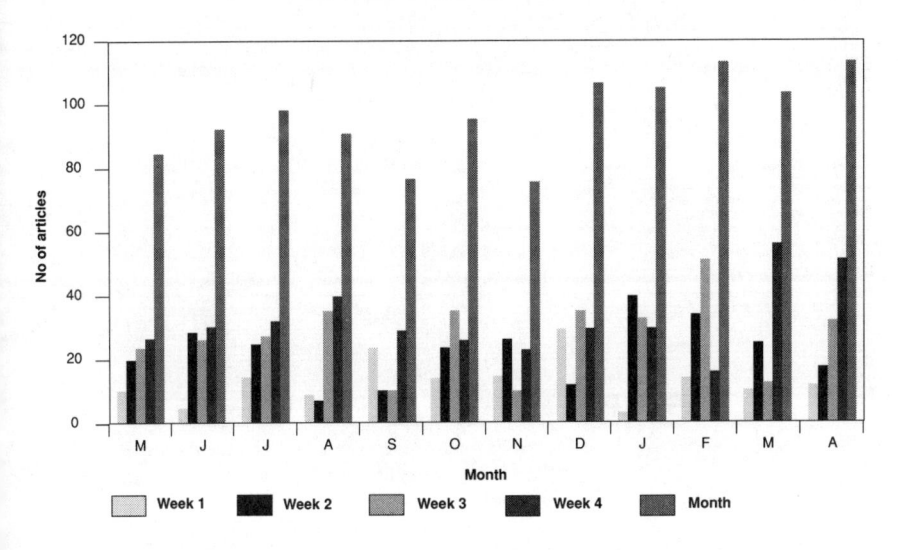

Figure 2.6a) Cuttings received by week and month

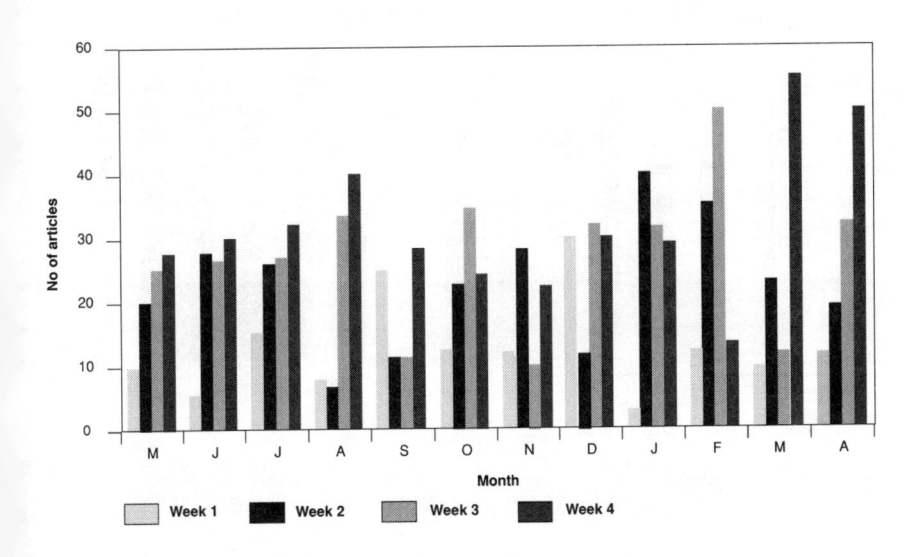

Figure 2.6b) Cuttings received by week

daily or weekly intervals makes measuring difficult to understand. In Figure 2.6 a) and b), the difference between weekly reporting and monthly reporting is shown. While in the upper chart, weekly reporting does not seem to show any reliable trend, the same statistics reported monthly show trends quite clearly.

37

Evaluating Press Coverage

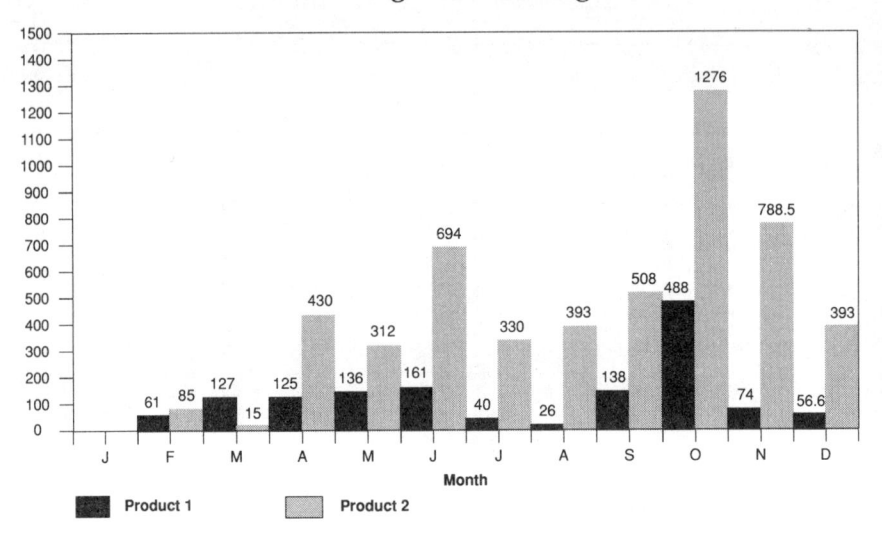

Figure 2.7 Column centimetres published

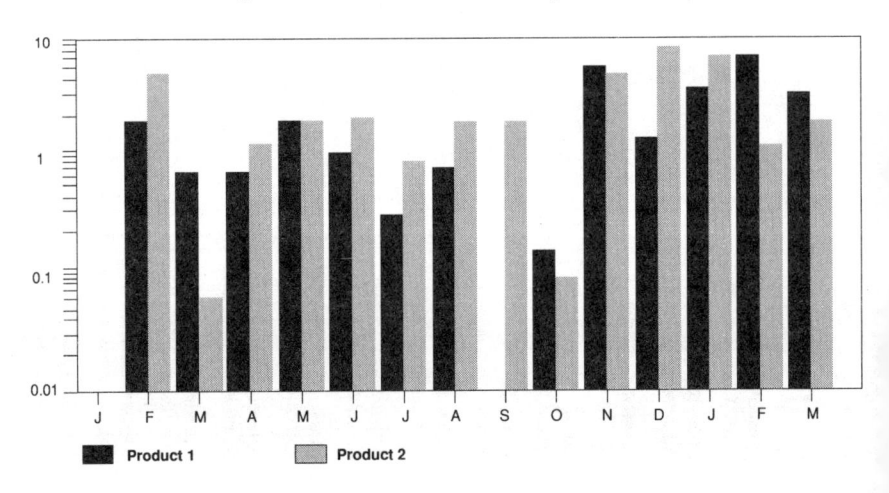

Figure 2.8 Average articles per press release

Assuming all the relevant publications have been assessed, coverage gauged in area or ccm is quite an important measure as:

- it gives an idea of the level of authority and impact it conveys to the reader;
- trends and comparisons give a clue to the best writers and the level of acceptance for different styles and content for press releases and briefings;

38

Measuring Coverage

- it also tracks how much space publications are prepared to devote to a subject when all competitive but related coverage is taken into account.

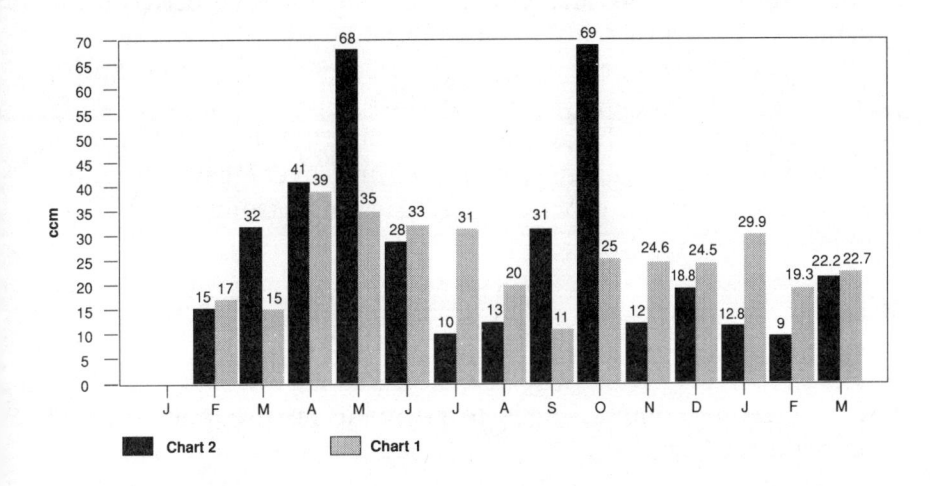

Figure 2.9 Average article length (column centimetres)

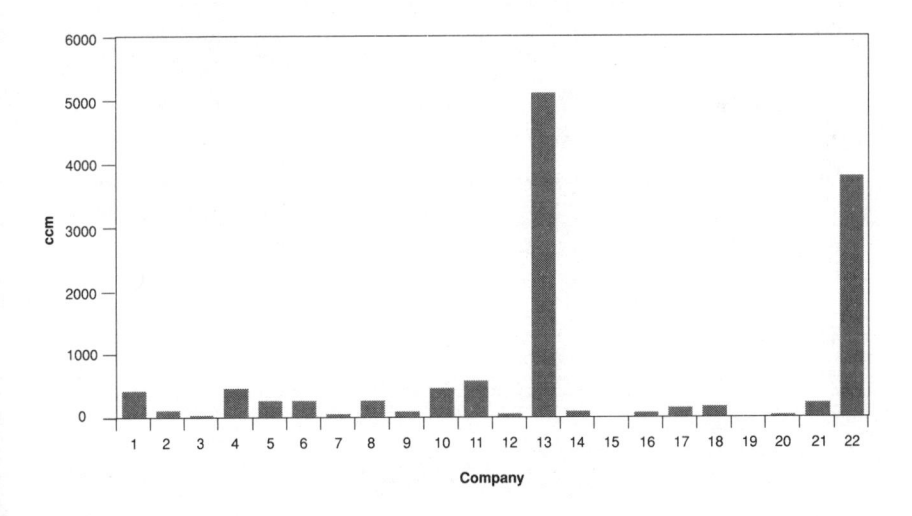

Figure 2.10 Industry coverage column centimetres of top 20 companies and others, 1990

Each of these issues is dealt with in depth later in this book but it is sufficient to say that a straightforward charting system provides useful data from which good management decisions can be made.

Evaluating Press Coverage

Figure 2.6 (page 37) shows a simple chart of coverage over a number of months which becomes valuable when making absolute judgements about the volume of coverage a client is receiving.

In Figure 2.7 a measure of comparative coverage between the client and competitors provides comparable absolute coverage.

In Figure 2.8 average coverage per article gives some indication of the quality of the coverage. In the chart we see how a lone case study or feature increases the average article length for a single month before the average again falls to its base-line coverage which, in this particular campaign, came from a series of personnel and order announcements.

Comparing coverage

An interesting comparison is to be made against one or more competitors.

In Figure 2.9 the average ccm per cutting is charted and we can see a rounded press campaign with an even distribution of different types of story marked (1). A competitor (2) shows little evidence of a sustained programme of press activity. Analysis suggests a competitor with low writing skills. Figure 2.10 shows the total coverage for all the leading companies in this particular industry. The conclusions are obvious.

Such charts can be used to judge and quantify press relations effectiveness, to identify the success of competitors and to formulate the strategy required to produce superior coverage.

3

Measuring Impact

Published material on content analysis should be basic reading for all students of public relations as methods of evaluating press coverage and its effect are so important to the subject. In the worst case, the absence of analysis can be likened to issuing a press release to a wide range of publications without looking for or noting the results. In a more structured environment content analysis will help identify the relevant journal and journalist for more focused distribution and will identify the attitudes of the journalist beforehand. In analysing the effect after publication, a similar assessment can be made. While some campaigns will call for massive press release distribution to numerous writers (motoring writers seem to abound and are an example of the potential for wide distribution), it is through this pre and post evaluation that such distribution can be justified and relevant.

Equally, the irritation of many journalists at being the target of much press release paper is symptomatic of poor evaluation by press offices. All too often a press office will assume a connection between a story and a publication which is beyond the comprehension of the editor.

Almost every press officer will have run a press campaign which seems to have had no impact on the media. With careful analysis the reasons can be identified.

A case in point was an attempt to take a very advanced hi-tech product to market via the media. Acceptance by the press was abysmal although competitor coverage was very much in evidence. It was content analysis which identified this failure and also identified the bylines which frequently occurred. A little investigation showed that the editors were not sufficiently up to date to note the relevance of what was being sent in. They depended on non-staff writers to make these judgements. By targeting the specialist writer, the campaign suddenly took off and was successful.

A view of the competition is also provided by contract analysis. GEC CEGELEC, an electronics company, was in the habit of taking about 7 per cent of all mentions against its six principal rivals. In October 1991 it jumped to over 20 per cent which it sustained into the following month. With only a limited number of publications covering the subject, other companies lost their share of coverage, which baffled them somewhat. One of the competitors believed that it was the quality of press releases issued that accounted for the decline of coverage. The one company taking content analysis seriously knew this not to be so and took a strategic view of how it could retain its normal high share of coverage.

The strategic and tactical role of content analysis is critical to the success of press relations programmes. Since straightforward measures of press effectiveness are not common features of press relations reporting, we shall now examine some of the basics which are more commercially applicable.

The editorial message

The value of editorial coverage differs greatly from that of advertising (see Figure 3.1). The act of faith shown by a publication in printing a story is very significant and is one that grows with the amount and quality of the coverage provided. There is a not only a distinct emotional advantage in editorial coverage but a considerable subliminal effect on the reader.

A statement of importance

The amount of space given to an article is an editor's statement of the importance of a story to the publication and, by inference, the importance a reader should place on the article. (See Figure 3.1). During even a cursory glance at a page-long item, key information will be noted and a split-second decision made as to whether the piece is of interest to the reader. Appearance is, therefore, vitally important if a column is to hold the reader's attention. The skills involved in shaping a page and presenting different stories with eye catching headlines are not to be under-estimated.

Measuring Impact

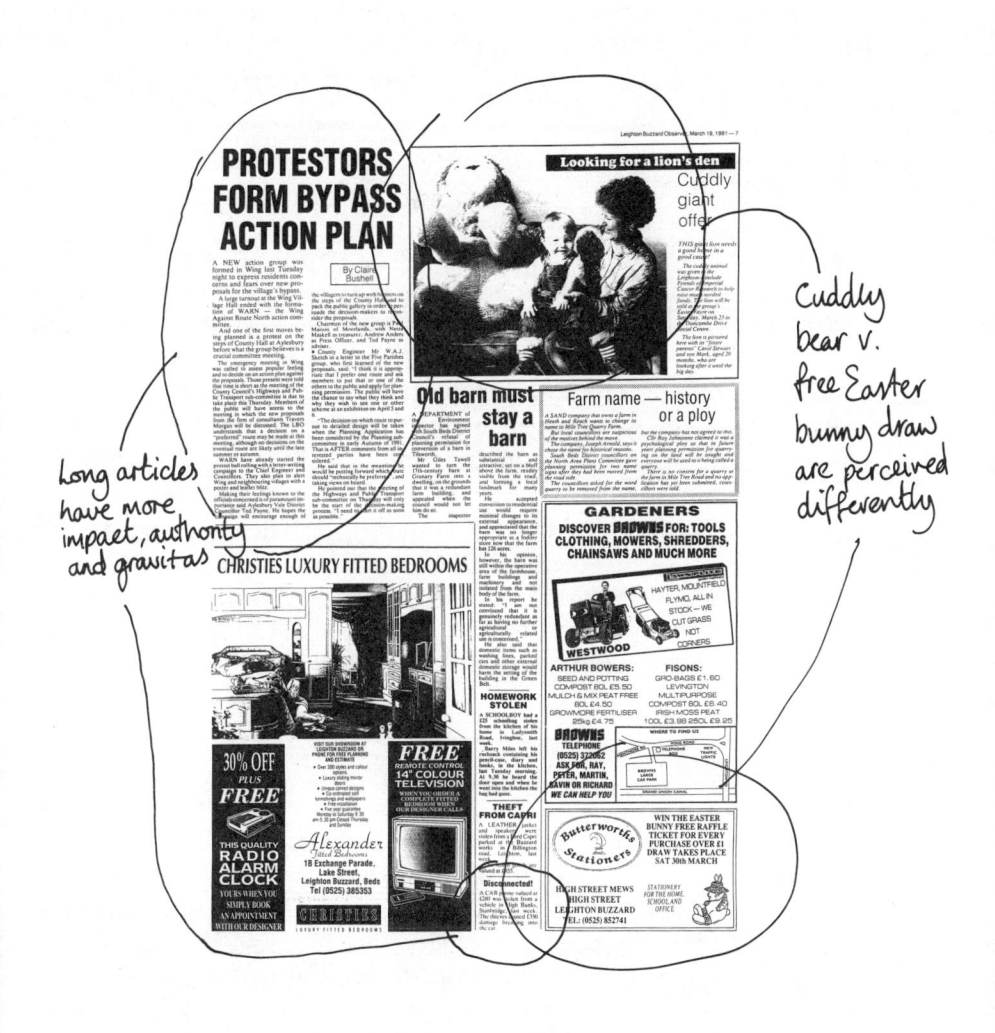

Figure 3.1 Advertising and editorial perceived in different lights; significance of article size

(Annotations: "Long articles have more impact, authority and gravitas"; "Cuddly bear v. free Easter bunny draw are perceived differently")

Eye-catching content

Content can have a poisitive or negative impact on the reader. If that first paragraph cannot capture the reader's attention or if the article becomes difficult, complicated or boring, concentration is soon lost. Successful publications will either junk or rewrite press releases which fail the same test.

Position of the page and on the page

Page position also has impact. Front-page news is powerful but after that page relevance differs from publication to publication. Unfortunately finding a grading common to all is not possible and, unless the media sample is small, it is the message and readership profile which economically dictates page position value.

An item can be juxtaposed or placed among other articles which may influence its impact on the reader. This contextual view is frequently the subject of heated debate. In Figure 3.2, context analysis is difficult, since surrounding articles are frequently excluded from press cuttings. Of course, there are occasions when context is important, for instance when the key word is included in an article (Figure 3.2) covering a wider subject or when it seems to have little relevance to the publication or readership.

Timing

The right article at the right time is immensely valuable. The converse is also true! (Figure 3.2).

To allocate value to these impact creators, it is vital that they are measured against a recognisable yardstick. The temptation is to measure coverage against advertising (see Figure 3.3), a convenient method since publications have an advertisement rate which, on the face of it, provides comparable value. It is a spurious measurement for a variety of reasons which will be discussed later.

The worth of assessing all these distinctions is not open to question at this point but monitoring all the aspects of impact is complex and requires extreme commitment. As a result it is expensive.

Measuring Impact

Timely Coverage — **PROTESTORS FORM BYPASS ACTION PLAN**

Key words in context

Juxta-position can be important for how articles are read in context.

Figure 3.2 Position on the page; key words in context; the importance of timing

Evaluating Press Coverage

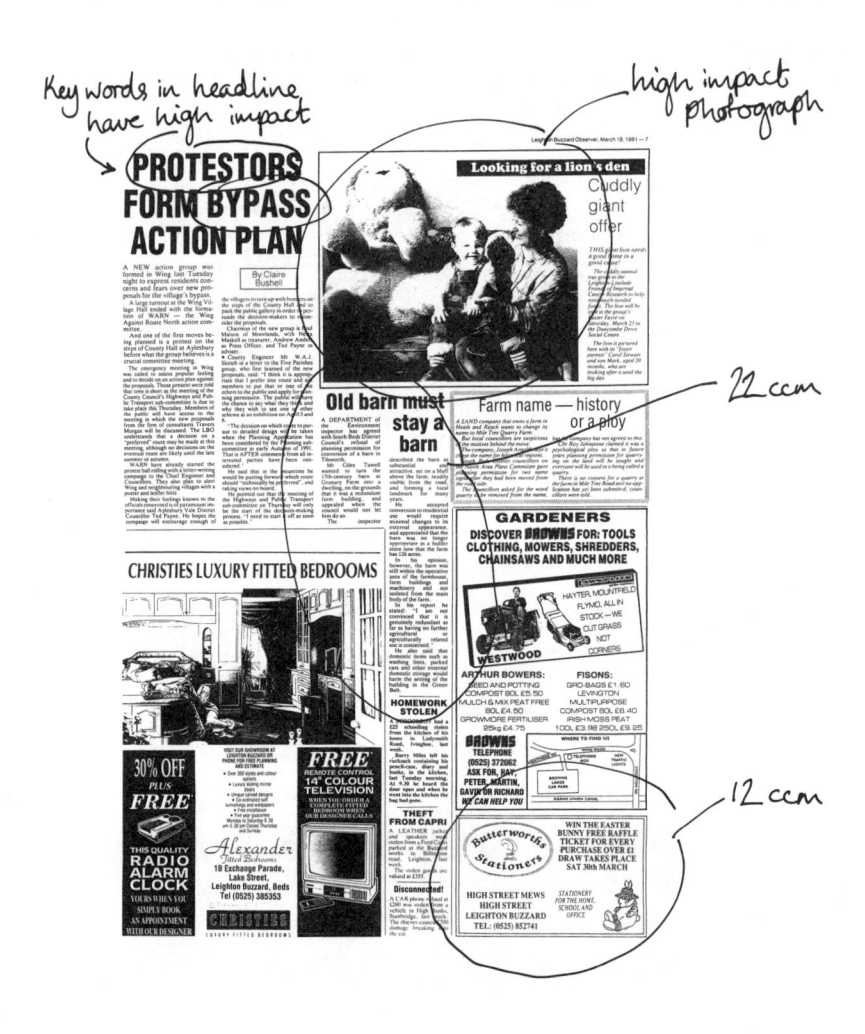

Figure 3.3 Comparing editorial and advertising; headlines and photographs

Easily measured impact

Impact which is relatively easy to assess from various statistics can demonstrate the force of coverage.

Headlines

A banner headline containing the client's name is an appealing prospect and deserves a high impact rating (Figure 3.3). If the ensuing article is a lengthy one it will convey importance, authority and weight.

Photographs

There is no doubt that a striking photograph has great appeal and can sell a story in a major way. Equally a poor photograph, an unflattering or badly lit shot can do harm to the success of the press coverage.

Length of article

It is quite simple to measure length and, as in the case of Figure 2.4, relative impact of different article lengths. They can be evaluated by allocating them to one of three catagories:

- Over 50 ccm;
- between 25 and 49 ccm;
- less than 25 ccm.

In the example of Figure 3.2 the measure usually amounts to less than one full column, two columns and over three columns in a typical four-column spread. It is valid in a campaign where most of the coverage was targeted to trade and technical publications, and proved to be quite an effective measure of authority for a company looking for press coverage conveying prestige beyond its market share size.

More complicated measures

These include column width which has to be used in conjunction with some other measure, typically column centimetres. In this instance, a column area rating is obtained. An article 36 ccm long, set on two 4.75 cm columns gives 342 square cm of coverage (Figure 3.4).

Alternatively the percentage of the page covered can be examined. This however, is quite difficult (Figure 3.5). Properly, such a measure should look at the percentage of page available for editorial to avoid confusion with advertising, a different type of message carrier. A measure of relative space given to the article, combined with a measure of all other editorial and advertising on the same page will give us a direct proportion of the article impact. Such an assessment is difficult and expensive to measure and quantify. Equally, space measurement can involve a lot of very small pieces where context in the page is probably important and requires considerable analytical skills to evaluate.

For most practical measurement, simple and inexpensive to measure, column centimetres takes a lot of beating.

To be sure of consistency, the rules for measuring article size have to be properly articulated. If, for example, the headline spreads over more than one body-text column then the column centimetre rating for the headline is simply the height of the headline multiplied by the number of body text columns. The column centimetres for each photograph are calculated in the same way and thus the ccm value for any article or cutting is simple to calculate.

There are, although not yet common currency, other important measures which can tell us a great deal. For the purposes of this book, columnar spread, percentage of page, position on the page and position of the page in the journal have too many areas of doubt to be considered in depth. Important as they are, being difficult to measure and quantify means that other measures which are simpler to define and record are more appropriate.

Impact rating

Put simply, impact can be measured only by speaking to readers and speculating on the effect of combinations of headlines, photographs etc, which is, strictly speaking, only a measure of presence. None would gainsay that a big article on the front page of a high circulation national newspaper will have greater impact on more people than a small article deep inside. Equally a small article in a relevant newsletter can have great impact although only circulated

Measuring Impact

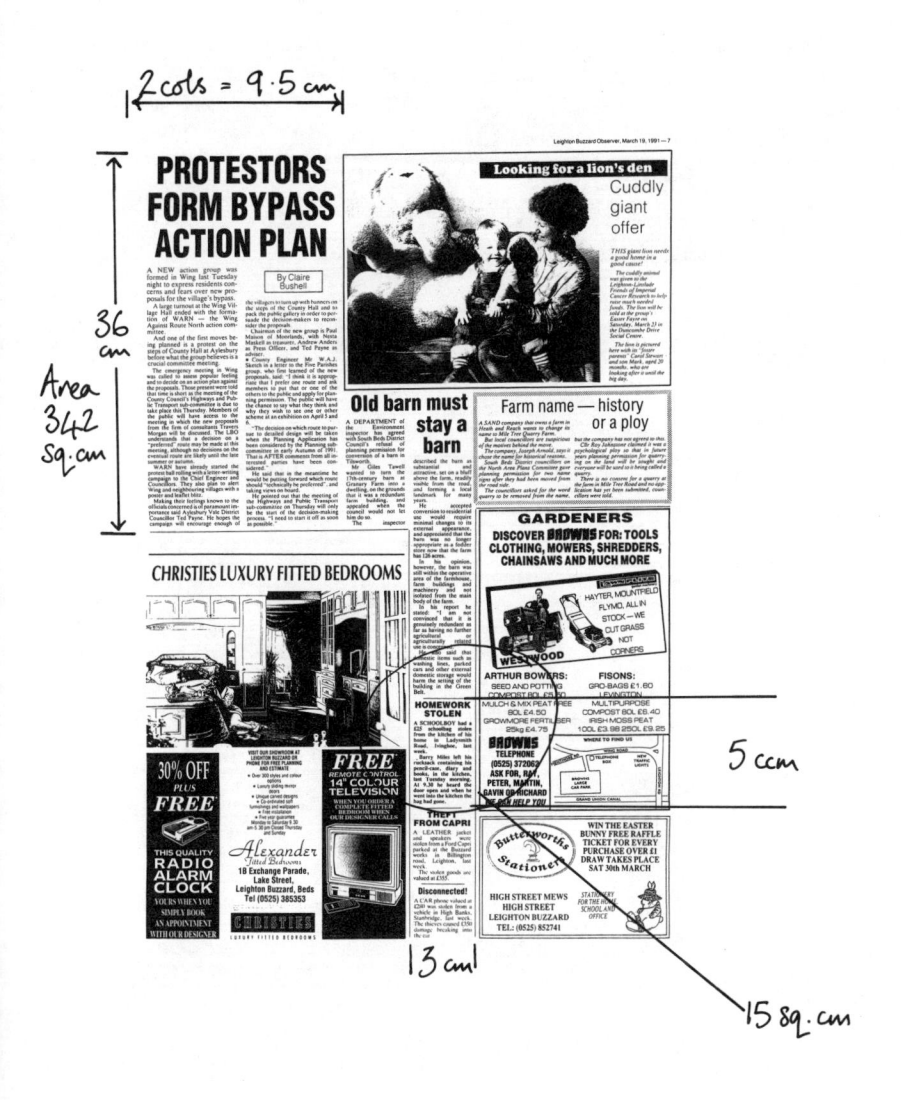

Figure 3.4 Measuring column centimetres and area

Evaluating Press Coverage

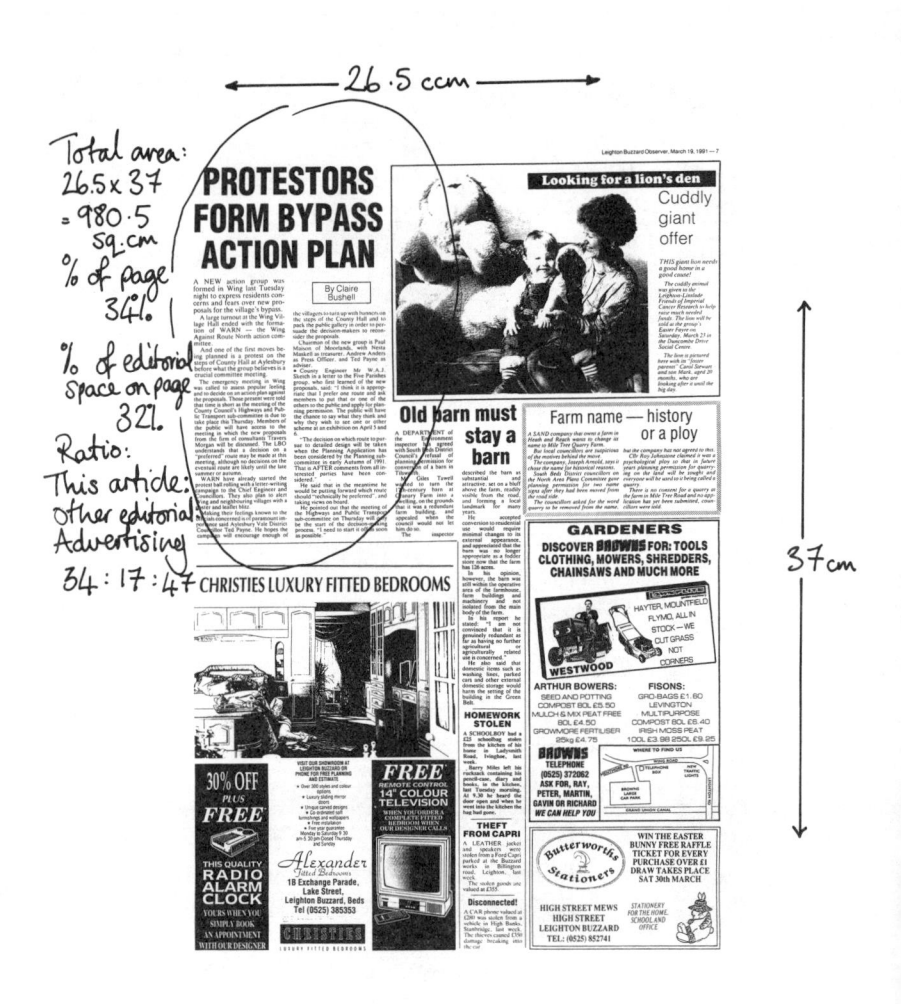

Handwritten annotations:

Total area:
26.5 × 37
= 980.5 sq.cm
% of page: 34%

% of editorial space on page: 32%

Ratio:
This article : other editorial : Advertising
34 : 17 : 47

Figure shows a newspaper page (Leighton Buzzard Observer, March 15, 1991) with article "PROTESTORS FORM BYPASS ACTION PLAN" by Claire Bushell, along with other items: "Looking for a lion's den — Cuddly giant offer", "Old barn must stay a barn", "Farm name — history or a ploy", "GARDENERS — DISCOVER BROWNS FOR: TOOLS CLOTHING, MOWERS, SHREDDERS, CHAINSAWS AND MUCH MORE", "CHRISTIES LUXURY FITTED BEDROOMS", "HOMEWORK STOLEN", "THEFT FROM CAPRI", "Alexander Fitted Bedrooms", 30% OFF PLUS FREE ad, and "WIN THE EASTER BUNNY FREE RAFFLE" from Butterworths Stationers.

Dimensions marked: 26.5 cm (width) × 37 cm (height)

Figure 3.5 Area comparisons for impact assessment

50

Measuring Impact

to a handful of people. However, to gain some concept of the impression most likely to be made a number of 'impact' measures are used and such measures assume higher impact as a result of more dramatic presence on the page.

Some companies put together an 'impact off the page' rating. For example, full page exclusive coverage with a name in a headline and a photograph is rated as having the greatest impact, while a single mention of the company name has the lowest. There are areas of press relations where this coverage is all-important and achieving one such article in a key journal is the essence of the whole campaign.

These kinds of measure may need a lot of analysis. For example, the size of headline or photograph in proportion to the article length needs detailed assessment and specialists are essential to interpret likely effectiveness.

For most campaigns a rating based on achieving exclusivity; full page coverage; a name in a headline; or a photograph, or any combination, should suffice. One point awarded for each element and an extra one for getting all four would give an adequate measure for a sizeable campaign where such occurrences are frequent.

A report such as the one illustrated by Figures 3.6 and 3.7 shows how the results can be presented. This shows how a campaign was measured against competitors and was used to gain an agency account.

This type of coverage is all very well if it is beneficial to the client. A discussion of the relative merits of good, bad and indifferent coverage is given in chapter 6.

Evaluating Press Coverage

	Client			Principal competitor		
	Actual	Factor	Count	Actual	Factor	Count
Exclusive article						
% of page						
100%	1 ×	15 =	15	1 ×	15 =	15
> 66%	1 ×	8 =	8	— ×	8 =	0
> 33%	2 ×	7 =	14	4 ×	7 =	28
< 33%	1 ×	6 =	6	2 ×	6 =	12
Exclusive mention	1 ×	4 =	4	12 ×	4 =	<u>48</u>
Total			<u>47</u>			<u>103</u>
Non-exclusive						
attributable share in ccm						
> 75%	1 ×	8 =	8	—		
> 50%	2 ×	7 =	14	—		
> 25%	2 ×	6 =	12	4 ×	6 =	24
> 10%	1 ×	3 =	3	2 ×	3 =	6
> 5%	2 ×	2 =	4	5 ×	2 =	10
< 5%	4 ×	1 =	<u>4</u>	11 ×	1 =	<u>11</u>
Total			<u>45</u>			<u>51</u>
Name in headline						
	3 ×	6 =	<u>18</u>	3 ×	6 =	<u>18</u>
Total			<u>18</u>			<u>18</u>
Photograph						
	1 ×	7 =	<u>7</u>	3 ×	7 =	<u>21</u>
Total			<u>7</u>			<u>21</u>
Total			**117**			**193**

Figure 3.6 Ascribing values to measures of press articles

The value of targeting

When niche marketing, the press officer will often be involved in obtaining coverage for a product out of context; full marks when this is achieved! Much case study and application story writing for the media is aimed at opening up niche markets. Persuading a food

Measuring Impact

magazine, for example, to cover transport may seem impossible, but if the topic chosen is a case study about speedy distribution of fresh produce the opportunity exists to have the article about transport covered out of context. If this can be achieved it is 100 per cent on target.

Core Publications Effectiveness

Total Articles

Impact measures achieved Advantageous mentions	Month one	Month two	Month three	Month four	Total
1. Exclusive articles		1	1	1	3
2. Full page (all of editorial space available)	1	1			2
3. Name in headline	1	1	2		4
4. Opportunities to read (10,000)	4	6	6	8	24
5. Photograph	1	1	1	2	5
Delivery score & circulation total	7	10	10	11	38
Quality of delivery	3	4	3	2	18

Figure 3.7 Method of assessing message delivery effectiveness in core publications

Coverage can have the absolute reverse effect if, for example, this hypothetical article is used in context to highlight poor service, complete with a photograph of a dirty truck in a muddy transport yard.

Most press campaigns, however, are not designed around one-off articles and impact is achieved over a planned campaign period. Measures of coverage such as average article length provide a very good indication of impact over a period of time (see Figure 3.5 on page 50).

As with all public relations activity, each of these measurements is valid only with effective targeting. Having fantastic impact values in the wrong publications is unwise and in some instances can be downright disasterous. One extreme example is when coverage of a single fire bomb incident in one shop of a chain gets national coverage.

The right media

There is a measure which is called the 'language of success'. It has been used in the UK to define the appropriate reach of different media. In this measure it is said that radio or television is more effective in reaching, say, a national audience but that regionally the local press will be a better medium for carrying a particular message.

Impact values using this method are quite well defined when selecting media and when measuring how effective targeting has been.

In later chapters we look at the use of media houses in assisting with the selection of journals for a campaign. If a measurement of impact also includes a measure of 'language of success', then weighting can be applied for added impact, particularly for carrying consumer messages. A view of good, bad and indifferent coverage, exclusivity, photographs and so forth has to be included if this added circulation reach measure is to be valid.

A method for achieving this added impact measure is to identify the important publications as key message carriers and to compare coverage obtained in them with total coverage for the campaign or programme. When this is tracked on a regular basis, a view of audience reach (effectiveness of targeting) can be made.

Having looked at impact in some detail we have to consider its relevance. Is it important and is it a measure of value? The answer is a very definite Yes. The quality of coverage is critical to the success of every press relations campaign. If articles are not read or are read in a negative light, then you will fail.

To compare your impact against some other coverage may be satisfying but, more to the point, it has a proportionate additional value. If there are two campaigns with equal numbers of cuttings but one has a greater impact, the benefit is obvious. By selecting appropriate impact ratings where effective comparisons can be made, a very accurate evaluation will result.

4
Monitoring the Output

We have, so far, assumed that coverage has already been achieved. Monitoring, however, must take place before a single word is published. The discipline to implement a simple routine will have a profound effect on future press work, and knowing what went into the media cauldron is always important.

Keep a press list

The good press relations officer already adheres to these simple management ground rules, but they always bear repeating:

- keep a simple press list;
- label each release clearly;
- include contact and follow up points.

The press/media list used for each release or project should include the following information:

- date of issue;
- time of issue;
- journal name;
- name of journalist/editor sent to;
- telephone number of journal;
- fax number of journal;
- address of journal.

In addition, media lists should include a brief summary of the release, including the subject (eg the product etc).

Reference press releases

It is usual practice to give each release a reference number to allow easy identification, retrieval and cross-referencing. Generally these numbers will include a code for client identification, type of release, writer's name and a sequential number.

Requests for additional information about the release will lead the executive immediately to the correct piece of coded work. More importantly, the code will allow any piece of published work to be identified with its source.

Reference press meetings

Conversations and meetings with press people can be recorded in a contact report with similar references. These, however, will include what the journalist was told, what the journalist said and details of other information provided.

The benefits of labelling include:

- good simple systems allow anyone in the press office to deal with enquiries;
- easy archiving and retrieval of all output work;
- journalists and press contacts, other press offices in your company and so on are able to refer to the release/briefing without confusion.

But the biggest advantage comes when we want to judge coverage for a campaign; undoubtedly, output will have its effect and press clippings will arrive.

Match cutting to source

As soon as practical it will be important to match the cutting to the source for the story as this is one of the basic effectiveness-monitoring techniques.

Monitoring the Output

EXEL
LOGISTICS

In the news ....

FINANCIAL TIMES
THE GROCER
MOTOR TRANSPORT
Retail Week

Prepared by ... COUNTRYWIDE

Figure 4.1 Effective monitoring by Countrywide Communications

For most press work this source can be matched to a press release issued or a press contact report and this is where careful output labelling will be most useful. A system used by Countrywide Communications illustrates how effective such monitoring can be and an illustrative example is provided in Figure 4.1 and in Appendix 3 (pages 218-31).

There are software systems matched to media lists (Romeike & Curtice launched one in 1991) which can integrate this information or it can be maintained on a press office database.

In some cases, knowledge about the source of a story is very important. There are occasions when it is vital to find out where a journalist obtained his information. If the source is from press releases issued or press briefs given, obtaining the source is only a matter of cross-reference. It is easier to achieve if the strategy outlined above has been adopted. It is also easy to discover if the journalist has other sources.

Sources

An added benefit derived from this report of output from the press office and the published article is the ability to measure the effectiveness of the writing and targeting of such media contact. It will be immediately apparent which agency/in-house writers and releases have been successful in gaining coverage and in which journals. The example kindly provided by Countrywide shows how this consultancy approaches the subject.

Journalists

Knowing the volume and nature of coverage provided by a journalist who may be reported or syndicated in a number of journals may be critical to the success of a campaign. In our measurement system, this shows the benefit of noting bylines.

Spokespersons

In yet another instance, a spokesperson or third party, such as a campaigner or politician, may provide the words or writing which stimulate journalists and press coverage. Knowing who these people are and what effect they have on a campaign can be very important.

At the end of the day we are looking for key words or phrases such as names, brands, products, issues, places and photographs. These are then attributed to the efforts of the press office or some other institution affecting the press.

Assignment of press releases and briefings

Finding the source of a story can be perplexing for people not normally involved with the account. The easiest method of identification is when a photograph is published. After that names of companies, people and products narrow down the search and it does no harm for the person who wrote the press release to identify his or her own work, which is quicker still. The problem is that some stories can have a lifetime of over a year. Journalists' computers keep information for a long time and some copy pops up not so much as mouldy news but positively spectral and takes some tracking down.

By establishing and using a simple system you will end up with a list of articles issued, a list of contacts with journalists and lists of the articles derived from both. Some systems can be quite complex but if they are easy to use will be of great value. For example, Figure 4.2 shows that from an analysis of 82 publications, the information derived can be extensive.

Content and style

All press coverage depends on content and style; simple monitoring will demonstrate only basic effectiveness. While the uninitiated may insist on a particular type of story, for example an order announcement to achieve an objective such as confidence in the company, the practitioner can quickly respond with counter arguments about storyline mix by proving that more mentions and authoritative (longer?) articles about product features (often with an eye-catching headline or photograph) have been achieved.

Tracking will quickly show the importance of storyline mix, how well the mix is being achieved and the relative impact of different stories on editorial decisions as to whether to publish or not. In some instances audience research will have already identified the type of story which will be most effective and with such targets it will be possible to ascertain whether or not the campaign is delivering the relevant story or story type to meet campaign objectives. Most stories are worth thousands of pounds to the image of the client (some are worth hundreds of thousands). Being able to identify the effort required to obtain the coverage and its effect in terms of appearances and impact is great news, both for the consultant and the client.

Evaluating Press Coverage

6 - SUBJECTS RECORDED

(Mobile) plant theft
AITT & truck safety
AJ Mechanical Handling Group
ART Telecommunications
Accident report
Alan Nash (HD, Hamech)
Atlet British Metal story
Atlet LPL order picker
Attachments
B&B Attachments
BKC Delco order announcement
BKC Dominator
BKC Range with Ford engines
BKC deal with Curtis Inst
BKC orders increase
Belotti reach stacker
Chassis Pacer
Clarion & Clark used trucks
Clark lift trucks/Clarion
Clark sales in Australia
Cleco
Cleco Bison PC narrow aisle
Cleco used trucks
Contact Attachments
Contract Engineering
Crane Scales Magnum
Crane Scales attachments
Crown Company Profile
Crown EPC pallet transporter
Crown PTH Series
Crown TS turret sideloader
Croown TSP
Crown Thomas Cork application
David Kerr (Crown HD)
Davy Morris AGVs
Deca pallet transporter
Desta range
Driver in court
E V Leonard range
Eagle FLT from Wilmat
Electrolux Constructor
Electrolux Hi-Lift
Electrolux VNA Range
Fiat Dunlop Cox delivery
Fliat Goodyear application
Fiat Venture Pressing story
Fiat appoints SFS as dealer
Fiat order by Gates Rubber Co
Fiat / Goodyear application
Fielden Engineers attachments
Fork Truck Centre used trucks
Fork Truck Hire Association
Fork Truck Safety
Fork truck Safety
Forklift Tyres Sales Ltd
Global buys Impact
Greenpar Connectors
Hallam MH attachaents
Hamech
Hamech R5 reach truck
Hamech electric range
Hamech electric trucks
Hamech used trucks
Handling Analysis
Handling Analysis attachments
Hans H Meyer attachments
Harvey Plant
Harvey Plant/Still/Courtaulds
Hyco reach stacker
IMM training courses
Industrias Luna reach stackers
JCB RTFL introductions
JCB RTLT
Japanese lift truct cartels
John Finlay attachments
Jungheinrich
Jungheinrich HS pallet truck
Jungheinrich used trucks
Konatsu Z Series
Komatsu/Pimespo
LTE attachments
Lift Truck Safety/Brewing
Lift Truck Safety/Harvey Plant
Lift truck attachments
Lift truck financing
Lift truck safety

Manns Mechanical Equipment
Mettler weighing trucks
Moffet Mounty
Monitor Training
Narrow Aisle Jaguar CS
Narrow Aisle VNA trucks
Nissan Poupart delivery
OM Fantuzzi sidelift CH
OMF Fantuzzi 7-High ECH
PGS ro-ro truck
PR Forklifts used trucks
Powell attachments
Powell drum attachments
Pyroban Zone 2 trucks
Record British Rail delivery
Record Lift Trucks profile
Record range
Regentruck used trucks
Robur pallet stacker
SMC attachments
Salter Quik Tach attachent
Sanderson receivership
Scanlift attachments
Sidetracker SB/SH reach trucks
Sidetracker sideloader
Southworth attachments
Still BICC application
Still R20 range
Still Toshiba application
Still attachments at Toshiba
Technomec attachments
Telxon PTC portable terminal
Terminals on trucks
Titan lift trucks
Toyota
Toyota FBM electric frontlifts
Toyota Rentokil delivery
Toyota used trucks
Toyota/Inpact Fork Truck
Translift Benditruck
Venture Pressings Fiat fleet
Wilmat Power Driven Stacker
Wilmat attachments
Wilmat pedestrian range
Wilmat pedestrian truck

SOURCES RECORDED

Anne Edwards
Antoon Cooijmans
Barry Woledge
Bob Helbert
Bruno Kulick
Colin Watson (Yale)
Dennis White (Travis Perkins)
Frank Harker
Frank Harker (Falcon Dist)
G B Lovatt
G Lovatt
Geoff Grosset
John Arkell
John Ettling (Hutchings)
John Gilbert (Lansing-Linde)
John Kinchella
John Roley (Grace Dearborn)
Keith Dicerson
Michael Brooks (CPRE)
Michael Scotese
Mike Mellor
PPW Lyons
Peter Stoneley (Finning)
Ray Norris
Roger Cox
Steve Lyons
Tony Heaton (Edbro)
Tony Mesquita
Trevor Bowman-Shaw
Trevor Wood

6 - BYLINES RECORDED

Alex von Stempel
Andrew Baxter
Andrew Macleod
Charles Leadbeater
Geoff Bone
Henry Snell
Hugh O'Mahony

Jim Pearce
JRS "Dai" Carter
Jeremy de Souza
John Mullin
Mike Jefferies
Patrick Hennessy
Richard Thomas
Robert Thomson
Roy Holder
Sally Lambourne
Stephen King
Stewart Tendler
Trevor Bowman-Shaw

6 - STORY SOURCE

Publications recorded
Builders' Merchants News
Hire News
Aerospace Composites & Materials
Industrial Handling & Storage
Materials Handling News
Storage Handling Distribution
Glass and Glazing Products
Manufacturing Chemist
European Window on Industry
Works Management
Government Purchasing
Purchasing and Supply Management
Personnel Today
The Engineer
Machinery Market
FEN Factory Equipment News
Industrial Equipment News
What's new in Industry
Engineering Distributor
Food Production
Steel Times inc Iron & Steel
Welding & Metal Fabrication
Sewells Car Digest
Tyres & Accessories
Oil Packer International
Print & Paper Series
Concrete Plant and Production
Construction Weekly
International Construction
Project Plant
Project Scotland
Cargoware International
Container Management
Dredging & Port Construction
Motor Transport
Transport Engineer
Transport Management
Cargo Systems International
Freight Management and Distribution Toda
Transport Week
The Safety & Health Practitioner
Safety Management
Daily Express
Financial Times
The Sun
The Times
Evening Post
Coventry Evening Telegraph
Express & Echo
Grimsby Evening Telegraph
Hull Daily Mail
Birmingham Post
Bedfordshire Citizen Series
Bedfordshire Times Series
Leighton Buzzard Observer and Linslade Gazette
Kentish Times Series
Ormskirk Advertiser Series
Lincolnshire Free Press Series
Post Series Harborough

Figure 4.2 Typical analysis of 82 publications

Monitor content . . .

A simple count of articles mentioning the client and column centimetres attributed from each story issued (with perhaps the name of the writer and a definition such as: order announcement, technical article, case study or personnel story) will soon show how much coverage can be expected from a particular amount (and type) of effort.

Equally, the effectiveness of input into, say, editorial features can be assessed in comparison with case-study material issued to a selected journal or journals (and how quickly editors get fed up with printing the same article as a competing publication!).

. . . and style

Style is very important. Writing perfect prose is not always the answer to an editor's prayer. Some stories simply miscarry. Rewritten they will score all round the park. Tracking will identify quickly the effect of style and soon compel some stories to be rewritten.

In the trade and consumer press, effectiveness between different writers can be assessed. Between three writers there can be a difference in frequency of acceptance of stories by editors and the treatment given which will have an effect on the impact (length, name in a headline, etc) of the article and hence in the way it is presented on the page. Variations by any number of different types of measure can be as much as 25 per cent. Guess who gets the work!

Already tactical decisions can be made from very elementary information by matching output to the press coverage obtained.

Cost of measurement

There is a significant argument about the size of budget available for this kind of research and monitoring. The Cranfield School of Management has looked at the subject in a report commissioned by the Public Relations Consultants Association (January, 1990) and some of its conclusions and reported comments are quite depressing reading. Many public relations practitioners are very wary of measurement and many offer the excuse that clients will not pay. While they are not in the least happy with comparisons to

Evaluating Press Coverage

advertising spend as a bench-mark for the value of press coverage, simple statistics soon come into play.

Every client should ask for some financial measure or a measure by which coverage with effect on the business can be compared. The best value is when the least number of variables enters the system. For example, comparing press coverage with market share is far too vague although correlation of coverage with market share over time may be used in conjunction with other measures. The effects of

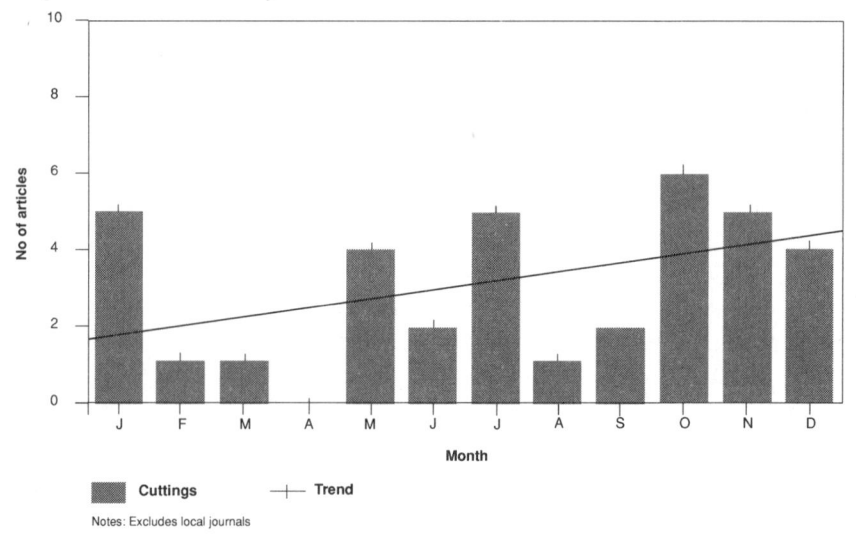

Figure 4.3 Unsolicited articles published

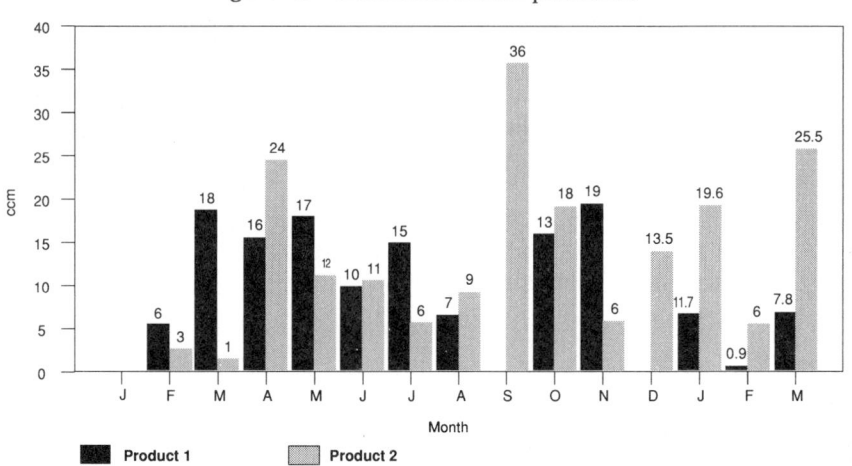

Figure 4.4 Column centimetres per enquiry

Monitoring the Output

advertising, sales effort, product suitability, and so on, all have impact on market share and press relations will be only a part of this mixture. On the other hand, the use of information issued in a press release by third parties to specify a product or an unsolicited mention directly attributable to the client is a valuable measurement of public relations effectiveness (Figure 4.3). A further example may also be the number of sales enquiries received (Figure 4.4) which is often compared to the cost of other promotional effort.

As long as like is compared with like there is every reason to use such comparisons (comparing the relative cost of enquiries derived from exhibitions and press coverage but excluding the cost of in-house time for both is thus meaningless). There are few press campaigns where a comparison is anything but positive.

A recent study (by Media Measurement Ltd, 1990-91) of all forms of sales enquiries received by a company (ie those generated by advertising, exhibitions, direct mail, product cards and press coverage) and all articles about the related industry, showed a distinct relationship.

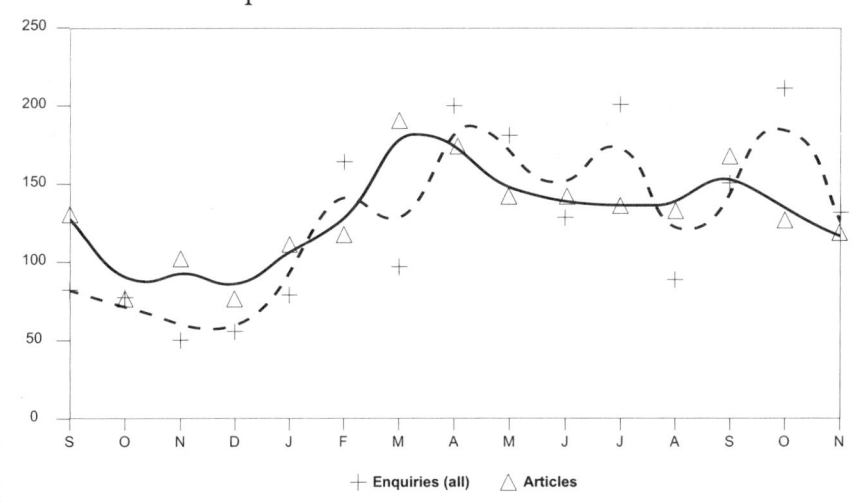

Figure 4.5 How enquiries follow share of coverage

There is a relationship when comparing all the coverage about the client and all its competitors across the whole industry and the client's enquiries as shown by Figure 4.5. In this graph we see a close relationship between articles as attributed to the industry (including the client) and the number of all enquiries received by the client. This shows that the media coverage over a 15-month period has

Evaluating Press Coverage

influenced awareness and, indeed, influences the audience sufficiently for the readers to act.

The relationship between share of coverage received by the client against all competitors in its industry and enquiries received as a result of editorial coverage, shown in Figure 4.6, was perhaps the most interesting outcome of this study. When 'Art' is the share of articles attributed to the client out of all articles published about its industry, 'ccm' is the share of column centimetres attributed and 'PR' is the number of sales enquiries directly attributable to responses from editorial coverage. From this it is reasonable to assume that there is a close relationship between share of coverage and impact on readers. The uncanny relationship between share of articles and press-coverage-generated sales enquiries identifies that a *high share* of coverage directly affects the number of enquiries.

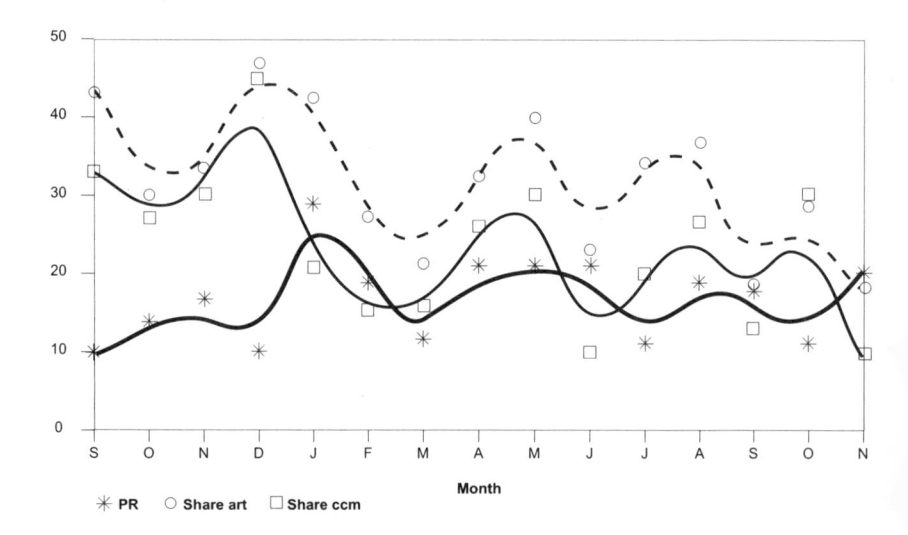

Figure 4.6 Enquiries as a result of editorial coverage

Here then is a quantifiable benefit which can be used to measure press coverage effectiveness. More work needs to be done on the subject but it will cause a number of 'diffusion of innovation disciples' to adjust some of their views about the impact of press relations. From this extensive and continuing study (there is always a distortion in the last month as the data is not complete), press relations managers will see that it is very important not to have a lot of coverage but to have a *high share* of all the coverage available before optimum impact is achieved. Or, to put it another way, an organisation spending money on press relations may well be wasting it if the objective does not include getting the lion's share. And failure to get the biggest share of voice may well be adverse by contributing to competition effectiveness into the bargain!

This finding, more than any other in recent years, favours the view that press coverage affects readership in a very direct way and to be half hearted about a press relations campaign is short sighted.

A case study

Another method of measuring press coverage effectiveness is based on a calculation used in 1988 for the trade press editorial versus advertising. It took the sum of all column centimetres of editorial coverage for a client and estimated the number of typical page lengths for typical industry journals. In this instance most journals had a page length equivalent to 75 column centimetres. Advertising space typically cost £1500 per page in the journals. From this it is possible to attribute a nominal value to the coverage achieved and include an additional nominal value for origination cost as follows:

$$\frac{\text{Total ccm}}{\text{average page size (ie 75 ccm)}} \times £1500 \text{ (average advertising cost)}$$

= space value

add

origination (nominally @ £2500 each 'page')

= value

In this instance the value was £580,000 for 11,000 ccm and the client was impressed with the figure!

Deeper analysis was more critical. This type of valuation is really meaningless for a variety of reasons. The editorial coverage, although impressive, was by this measure an expensive method for generating enquiries. However the consultancy took the same coverage and tracked it against advertising enquiries and competitors' coverage over 12 months. The client was reassured to discover advertising enquiry cost was reduced as editorial coverage increased and, as competitors had less coverage, the competitor advertising was probably relatively expensive because of the lower coverage obtained.

Attempting to give a monetary value to editorial coverage is virtually impossible but a value can frequently be attributable to the relative effect achieved through editorial mention.

In this case, to justify a press relations research budget of 7.5 per cent of total press relations expenditure ensured future coverage was as successful in volume as well as targeting. The alternative was guesswork.

Output v effect: the most important measure

Once an organisation uses content analysis, output of press releases, frequently perceived to be a measure of press office worth, becomes less relevant than effectiveness. One of the most important features of the above exercise is that the level of output dropped dramatically. The blanket approach to issuing press releases was quickly seen as a concept of comfort and although the relationship between issuing press releases and coverage is important and has a dramatic effect on editorial mentions, each release is more closely scrutinised for its worth than before. Ownership of press output is now much closer to home for both client and consultancy and is carefully monitored to maintain output to effectiveness ratios. The bottom-line cost has reduced for client and consultancy but effectiveness has increased.

5

Press-Prompted Response

For much press campaigning the objective set is to find an available forum which will generate response. So it is surprising that, knowing the power of the media, research into response generation is so scarce. Blanket coverage, in many respects, seems pointless. A newspaper or magazine full of material which provokes no response will have little value since our objective must always be to provoke.

Motives behind response

Before we launch into the area of response it is worthwhile looking at the motivation behind response and the success of the press in achieving it.

Basic responses can be reduced to three areas:

1   coverage of life's essentials – food, housing, clothing, earnings and jobs.
2   coverage relating to the family unit – children, education, sex and health issues.
3   coverage which concerns relationships – social opportunities, group activities, problem pages.

Reading the press will evoke responses ranging from mild interest to violence but measuring coverage to assess specific types of response is not practical. In the first instance, we must decide if press coverage, in itself, is sufficiently important to require all this attention.

If the press does have a profound effect on people, then it is relevant to ask to what extent and to invite a question on how to quantify magnitude. It is from such a view that debate moves to assess the value of press coverage.

The magnitude of response

A focused message appearing in just a few publications which have great influence on readers is infinitely valuable. There is much debate about whether press coverage alone cannot only change attitudes but patterns of behaviour.

The effect and impact of advertising is well researched but the arguments that the media merely brings information to public attention and action is stimulated by other influences is far too simplistic.

Where, for example, an ill defined need exists, the media can easily help in defining the need and provide access to the solution. Where peer pressure does not exert itself, the media can provide focus and in both instances will prompt action. If we return to Figures 4.5 and 4.6 in the previous chapter we see that without media intervention action does not take place whereas when the media is active people change behaviour.

If, without editorial coverage, a person does nothing and as a result of media coverage a decision to enquire prompts the reader to take action, it is self-evident that the media does change behaviour without another influence coming to bear. While this study of sales enquiries is not very profound it has more than a little validity and is the basis of considerable investment by industry and commerce.

Perhaps the findings of this small tracking sample are to some extent perceived common sense. If an industry is making a lot of noise people notice it and the level of enquiries goes up. If one contributor to all that noise shouts louder then it gets a higher proportion of the available enquiries. No doubt the combination of a variety of influences is more powerful and person to person contact, peer pressure and a host of other effects will be more telling.

Nevertheless, a message in a hundred inappropriate publications can have marginal or even negative value.

The question we are asking is, 'What is the effect of editorial matter?' Recent experience provides some clues.

Press-Prompted Response

Lessons of the Gulf War

The populations of many countries have recently been persuaded to accept the fact of war. Inter alia, this means that many of civilisation's sensibilities were set aside; the world was prepared for people to suffer and be killed. While it is accepted that civilisations accept the necessity of war and are in some sense prepared for it in justified circumstances, the case for going to war has to be made very thoroughly especially in democracies influenced by wide-ranging media, inexpensive and generally available mechanisms for communication and debating forums in abundance.

The Gulf War was an example of press influence over millions of people. Its influence was seen in its rawest state. In this instance knowledge about the country and its rulers was not generally well known. Radio, television and political exposure was muted and yet progressively in a small number of specialist publications and then in the heavyweight journals information and a view of the country, its governing regime and its aggressive ambitions were exposed. No other communication mechanism (such as radio or television) had significant influence until there had already been a major effect on public attitudes and motivations, except the press.

TV, radio and the press each had distinctive roles to play over a relatively short period of time. In something less than a year the West had moved from a position of ambivalence towards Saddam Hussein and Iraq to actual war. Radio and television were late in testing the intellectual arguments about the regime and the merits of war. The press, on the other hand, argued progressively towards such a conclusion over several months.

It is interesting to watch the interplay between these different media. While the press argued the case, it was the television pictures which provided the impetus and eventually took the initiative. In a very short time the press took us through all the processes needed to be at war. There was no other mechanism which could have influenced public opinion so effectively. Its influence was profound. Some concept of how the effect was felt by individuals whose sole involvement was to work in a factory making forgings is evident in the dole queues they now frequent. Customers whose knowledge of the involvement of a company with Iraq cancelled orders based on what they read in the press and, as we now discover, at Select Committee hearings in Parliament.

Evaluating Press Coverage

For the dispassionate outsider viewing the influence of the press from a different perspective, media influence was one contribution which affected many people and in many ways. On a more personal level, there was a direct and attributable influence which changed lifestyle and not for the better.

While one does not want to attribute too much influence to the press, nor to the media as a whole, the level of effect is all too often played down.

Two other examples of media effectiveness come to mind: Watergate, in which the media (Washington Post) opposed the consensus of the day and cultivated public opinion, and the Maxwell scandal in which the absence of media coverage until after the death of Robert Maxwell contained the disquieting views of a number of commentators and insiders to a clique whose members were not prepared or able to use the media and influence public opinion, regulatory bodies, Mirror Group employees and so on.

Editorial coverage cannot be evaluated in the same way as other methods of opinion forming and communicating. We know, for example, that some of the coverage of the Gulf War was inaccurate and misleading. We also know that the press was highly rated as a means of purveying information until television began its wall-to-wall coverage, after which public mistrust progressively crept in.

From specialist to mass-market press

If a small number of publications has real influence over opinions, what happens if the message is not passed through these publications but through other journals with only a secondary influence? Influential publications have a permanent need for originality and there is a constant requirement for publications to 'own' their individual approach. In addition, a key publication which merely reprints an argument is not providing the same stimulation for the reader. Thus, press relations must be precisely focused. This does not mean that coverage in tertiary publications is harmful; it can be very beneficial as background and is well known for its ability to pre-empt mass publications. Specialist magazines will give the key journal and journalist comfort that the subject matter is not too far fetched. What is important is that the issue addressed by a key journal is new and throws fresh light onto a subject.

Press-Prompted Response

Market Data Information in the USA presents a very good case for believing that publication in the specialist media can lead eventually to a story in the national press (*Organic Food Sales*, Market Data Enterprises, New York). John E Merriam contends that it is worth thinking about publications in terms of their readers. Thus, ideas about diet and nutrition are published first in technical journals. The coverage then moves through popular-science magazines and 'healthwise' newsletters to diet magazines, daily newspapers and finally mass-market magazines.

There is a reasonable consensus suggesting that stories in their original form have a half-life of about six months (at which time they have very little currency in either the trade or national press – ie 'yesterday's news'). Tracking studies by Media Measurement Limited (see Figure 7.2) below are typical and show the life of real stories in the press. John Merriam made the same point in *American Demographics* (February 1991).

The process by which stories emerge in a local, learned or technical publication and progressively move to wider-circulation publications requires added impetus on its journey. This impetus may be generated in akin or parallel media or other influences such as personal experience or other events. This cumulative effect overlays coverage in one medium with the next. The process is like the ripples created in a pond when a stone is throw into the centre. If no other disturbance occurs the ripples will fade away. If another stone is lobbed in the waves will begin to reach the shore and lots of stones will generate very choppy waters. In the analogy, the stone is the story and the pond, the press.

Thus a story with a half-life of six months has to progress from the technical publication to the national headlines within this duration or has to be 're-launched' to gain wider media acceptance. Evidence of tracking stories (in particular the circulation reach) would confirm that the impact of a feature in one publication can prompt coverage in another.

To cite, once more, the case of the Gulf War: serious UK publications did not take a major interest in the Iraqi issue until mid 1989. The initial coverage of internal atrocities had come out of the headlines a year earlier and the new approach by publications had involved issues of a peripheral nature. The only common element was distaste for the Baghdad regime. These early exploratory articles were less about the regime, concentrating on more salacious coverage such as bank scandals and shipments of arms and equipment.

Volume of coverage increased from the summer and rose to a crescendo immediately after the invasion of Kuwait in August 1990. Most of the impact on public attitudes was achieved in the previous three months.

This whole episode will provide academics with much food for thought and significant investigation is needed to learn enough about the subject for completely valid judgements to be made. We cannot be relaxed about the power of the press. It is a mighty part of everyday modern life. And if the press can so influence a nation, what is its effect in other fields? If it has similar effect elsewhere, how valuable is that effect when working for a client and how damaging when working against?

More powerful than advertising

Such measures cannot be compared to advertisement-prompted response; there is little evidence to suggest that advertising has an effect so profound that it will convince ordinary people to put aside normal sensibilities or that advertising has countered an editorial line in the public's eye. It follows that editorial coverage has its own value.

Why is it that such a powerful medium is seldom measured in any quantifiable way? How can we find out what its influence is, can and will be? In fact who watches these watchers? Surely it is the duty of the public relations profession, which claims to be interested in opinion forming and communication, to know and know very precisely and in quantified terms the nature of the media monster.

Knowing that the press is powerful, how can we assess press relations' effectiveness? We know that if there is a major issue, the press is overwhelmingly powerful. We know that it has considerable impact when the issue is relatively minor. Instinctively we can evaluate the relative level of coverage and the efficacy of different coverage. To be able to do so using the analytical technology available is only just now becoming popular.

Press influence is unique and requires a unique type of evaluation. We now need to look at some of the more common instances where we can find and benefit from press-prompted response. In essence, it is the individual publication which will engender the type and level of reaction to its coverage. Style and content has an all important role.

The *Sun*'s now famous 'Gotcha' headline during the Falklands war provoked all manner of basic emotional responses and caused endless comment in the British media. For its readers at the time, the headline fed the basic human instinct for survival. There was no other national newspaper which aroused the same passions (Figure 5.1).

Some measure of how impact will prompt action is seen in the huge sums raised for charities working among the starving in North Africa. One photograph alone is credited with changing national attitudes towards giving money to Ethiopia.

Information, attitude and behavioural change

The debate about the role of public relations has changed over the years. From a simple statement about a planned programme of providing information, to a role in changing attitude, to the current belief among many that public relations should affect behaviour, PR has progressively and self-indulgently moved towards greater importance in the hierarchy of economic, social and political life.

There is no doubt that the ambition of every publicist is derived from a self-interest which, in turn, means that someone is going to change attitudes. Failure to change attitudes means the publicity failed. There is, in reality, no such thing as 'neutral' news.

Behavioural change as a publicity-induced response

To be effective, publicity must motivate people. And highly motivated people act. Thus press relations is about behavioural change. However, behavioural change is dimensional and is characterised by the level of motivation behind the change in attitude that occurs, the scale of behavioural change and the force behind behavioural change.

Examining voting behaviour

The progress made in assessing voting habits can be used as an example to illustrate this. The original data collected and some of the

Evaluating Press Coverage

Figure 5.1 Style and content can provoke tremendous response. This headline is appropriate to the newspaper and also has hugely emotive impact

early methods of predicting election results were based on past voting statistics. The next phase examined voting intentions and improved the quality of prediction dramatically.

Today we would look at the effect of issues on the electorate to measure if they will override voting intention. Voting behaviour has a number of different expressions:

- a traditional voting habit can be maintained;
- a traditional voting habit can be maintained reluctantly;
- a voting habit can be changed into an abstention;
- more dramatically, it will result in a vote for an opposing political party.

There is, thereby, an element of measurable force in such behavioural change.

Measuring effect of editorial on behaviour

Our skills in measuring this force from the effects of press coverage and through cutting analysis are not sufficient – yet.

While identifying how successful a publication will be in tempting, say, an engineer to enquire about an automation product, the ability of the message to play on basic human needs and fears should be taken into consideration. If the engineer believes, from reading an article, that his knowledge about this product will affect his job or salary, he will enquire. Such content and style is important. In time, measuring press coverage will become sufficiently successful to test the motivation behind behavioural change. If a publication provides every encouragement to make a reader react, a greater response can be expected. Already we can measure some of these prompts towards changes in behaviour.

Initially an impact assessment is needed and earlier some examples of these were given. This is only part of the equation and rating coverage for beneficial, neutral and adverse will help come to some additional conclusions. But if other values are added a better view is obtained.

Measuring off-the-page response

In addition to some of the elementary aids to response mentioned earlier in the book, a series of questions can be asked when reading a cutting to ascertain if the reader is stimulated to act:

- Does the copy contain the address (or part of it)?
- The telephone number?
- A reader enquiry number?
- A response coupon?

The answers tell us how much an article will help in detecting a change in attitude on the reader's part.

This is not the best yardstick though, since it has no basis on which to gauge effect. The potential to generate enquiries from coverage measured in this way will at best show improvement or otherwise and is based on previous experience. However, if these measures are compared with a known yardstick such as competitors, a measure of how effective a campaign has been, in absolute terms, is available.

How to bring all these elements together is open to all manner of interpretation. For some, giving a weighting to each element and then combining them in some kind of response evaluation may be one answer but other methods are needed for validation. To have a mechanism which compares sales enquiries with press response ratings, or an opinion survey to authenticate the measures, will be helpful. At the moment it is unlikely that there is any completed research to provide the kind of answers we need. We can only hope that in each individual circumstance there may be a way of constructing press relations campaigns which are response-oriented in the same way (and even more effectively) as in the field of advertising.

A need for research

The research needed may well begin with the ability to compare each of the impact measures, ratings for good, neutral and adverse and the data on helpful text to assist the potential enquirer. Across all competitors, market research findings may show linkage. To be more precise a motivation test may need to be added to the sample of cuttings to see what effect 'Gotcha' has.

Press-Prompted Response

The prospects are interesting and may prompt the detailed research required in public relations which has already been applied to other promotional activities.

There is no doubt that many marketing people find it difficult to understand why press coverage does not generate enquiries like advertising. A glance at the requirements given above to generate response will give some clues. Equally, the marketing men have devoted far too little research to finding out how press relations activity can be a positive benefit in producing response and thus behaviourial change.

The potency of the media in influencing behavioural change is evident; imagine turning a peace-loving nation to war!

Many people question the morality of provoking response through media manipulation. Journalists would defend their independence to the death if they thought for a moment that the public relations profession was so devious as to use them to change behaviour. They do, of course, accept the advertisements on the same pages as editorial matter.

6

Attribution

In passing, assumptions have been made about attributing customers' names and key words to a press cutting. Oh! Were it so simple!

A glance at the front page of almost any national newspaper will show that many articles are composite productions from several journalists quoting various and often competing sources for information and in many instances the quotations will be broken up into a number of separate statements. For the enthusiastic press-cutting analyst this type of cutting provides the most interesting areas for measurement. Deciding on what is appropriate to measure and confirming that this selection is valid is fraught with difficulties.

In every instance the methods used will need to concentrate on the readership rather than the journal. The relevance of the journal is limited to its effectiveness as a medium, the reach into the audience and how much of what is written is believed.

Some idea of what can be researched comes from the Welbeck Golin Harris study of ten leading women's magazines (*Adding Life to Brands – Some Key Insights into How PR Works in the Consumer Press*, 1990).

By looking at the basic 'ingredients' of the publications:

- advertising;

- magazine-originated editorial; or

- PR-led editorial;

several conclusions were made. These are summarised below.

Attribution

> **Summary of key findings**
>
> - Editorial 'read' more than twice as much as advertising
> - Only marginal difference between 'reading' of PR-led editorial and magazine editorial
> - Shared feature and offer for payment highest 'read' PR editorial techniques
> - Offer requiring payment higher 'reading' than free offer
> - Advertorials 'read' more than advertising
> - Slimming and health highest 'read' editorial product category
> - Magazines do add believability to brand information included in editorial
> - Readers believe recipes highest as most worth keeping
>
> *Copyright Welbeck Golin/Harris Communications Ltd*

Style, or technique, also has a bearing. When all types of editorial are indexed at 100, 'offer for payment' scores 100, 'shared features' 96, 'exclusive features' 92, 'Free offers' 85, 'advertorial' 81 and so on. Even the subject matter has an influence. The subject of 'slimming and health' scored 144 in the Welbeck index and 'alcohol' 60.

With this kind of information available, some idea of how difficult it can be to set parameters for detailed content analysis is apparent. However, all is not lost. While you may be at a loss to know how to have as much influence on the readers of women's magazines as on those of slimming and health magazines if you are working for an alcohol product, other types of measure may be useful. For example, you may want to assess how effective coverage is between competing brands. Knowing that the readership will be less attracted to coverage in women's magazines than if the subject were about slimming and health, the impact of coverage compared to a competitor may be all that is required to achieve the press campaign objective.

An interesting observation of the Welbeck research is the belief of the readers in what they saw. Readers were asked, 'if (magazine X) mentioned a brand name, how much would you believe what was said about the brand?' The respondents had to score 1 for believing nothing and 10 for believing everything. The results were surprising in that one in three readers scored 8, 9 or 10. The average over all ten magazines was 6.5.

Knowing something of the journals that are being measured, their readership and effectiveness, some of the quantitative and later, qualitative measures which can help to assess how well the message is received can be studied. A number of techniques can help.

The usual method is to develop a coding system which allows attribution of a particular measure or measures. Often this will be a key word or issue to which values can be attributed. Thus when the key word is found it can be attributed to the type and relevance of the journal in which this key word appeared. It may be that we wish to identify the circulation and readership with the opportunity to read about this key word, the frequency of the key word, and so on.

Key words

When measuring press cuttings for effectiveness, you need to look for key words or phrases which are directly linked to the issues with which you are concerned. Usually, these will be words or phrases essential if the article is to be of interest to you.

For example, imagine that you handle the public relations account for a person called George Bush, who happens to be President of a country called the United States, and wish to monitor coverage related to the Gulf War. Key words to look out for could be 'George Bush', 'United States', 'Gulf War/Iraq', 'General Schwarzkopf' and 'Middle East peace moves'. Clearly, articles which do not contain these words may not be of interest to you or your client because there will be nothing to link the article to you, your client, his country or the issue of interest (the war). In this case the most important word could be 'George Bush' and as such this will be the *principal key word*.

Once you have ascertained whether the key words appear, you can measure how much of the article is attributable to each key word. There are several ways of achieving attribution in any article but the initial briefing and objectives are, again, critical.

For example the key word or phrase may be one such as: 'President George Bush' or 'Moves towards Middle East peace and stability'.

Attribution

Secondary attribution

But there will also be relevant *secondary words* which are not going to be directly attributable to the President or Middle East peace but which, when used, should be indirectly, or by inference, attributed.

To identify how attribution is made might include a measure of the number of words, column centimetres or proportion of the article directly referring to the key word or phrase.

For example:

> General Schwarzkopf said allied forces had stormed virtually untouched into southern Iraq.

can be directly attributed to the General but:

> President George Bush was expected to announce military victory in the Gulf War in a nationwide address early today as a White House Official said the final tank battle south of Basra was moving rapidly to a close

is much more difficult to attribute. The principal attribution is to a White House Official. The inferred attribution may be to President Bush but should not be given to him.

In this instance the brief has to be quite clear and almost always there will be a key word/issue and one or more secondary words in the search. Thus the principal key word may be: 'President Bush' and secondary words may include 'White House Official', 'The (US) Administration' and 'Pentagon'.

In most analyses it will be useful to identify the name of the spokesperson as a separate entry so that a progressive list can be assembled of people who regularly pass public comment on the client or issue; a 'movers, shakers and commentators' list.

Other notable key words

In much analysis there will be a need to attribute comment to other people and issues. These 'other notables' may be competitor companies or, in the case of the above example, another public figure. In such a case the *other notable word* (ONW) will not have a direct link with the key word/issue, but will more likely operate independently of the main key word.

As with the key word(s) it may be that there will also be further words to consider. To avoid confusion we will call them *tertiary words*. To continue our current example, another notable word could be 'Saddam Hussein' while its associated tertiary words could include 'Tariq Aziz', 'Republican Guard', and so on.

Hierarchy of key words

The four kinds of key word considered so far might be classed as follows:

1 The most important will be the *principal key word*.
2 This has words which are always to be exclusively associated with it which we call the *secondary key words*.
3 To be able to cover the subject thoroughly we are looking for a competitive reference or *other notable word*.
4 In turn, other notable words have *tertiary words* or expressions which will always and exclusively be associated with the other notable word.

Now a hierarchy for allocating coverage to be attributed to each key word, phrase or issue can be developed. This means measuring and comparing the coverage given to each and assessing the impact it receives.

In building this methodology it is very important to make assessment as objective as possible. It will be important for two assessors working on the same project to be trained to give attribution in the same way. Later you will see that it is equally important that assessors also reflect the audience perception as well.

Beneficial, neutral and adverse

This ability to attribute parts of an article to different types of key word is fine for measuring coverage but it is of paramount importance when assessing whether the coverage is beneficial, neutral or adverse (BNA) for the individual key word under consideration.

In the first sense the BNA attribution should be made to the individual key word or issue. An article could be seen as, on the whole, beneficial but, as in the George Bush case quoted, a sour note would be added if, in an article of 75 ccm, the last 2 ccm said:

> RIYADH – *Nine British soldiers were killed by 'friendly fire' from a US aircraft in Iraq, a British spokesman said yesterday.*

This is not to be confused with the main article and a 'beneficial' rating for the White House spokesman still stands. The added comment should be measured as a separate item of news.

This article provides an excellent opportunity to see how the attribution of beneficial, neutral and adverse has to be applied directly to the key word and should be read with an independent view for each. Thus in an article such as the Bush statement a BNA attribution to Saddam Hussein will need to be made as though it were Saddam Hussein looking for the measure of beneficial, neutral or adverse in the article.

As the data is assembled this technique will show how attitudes change over a period of time and by using well-qualified secondary and tertiary words the relative importance of individuals is seen to change.

In every instance attribution must be made to a *person*. It may be a White House spokesperson but it is not the White House. The reason for making this clear is to ensure that, as attribution becomes more important, it is the individual who will become the target for a public relations campaign and the closer measurement focuses on that person, the better.

Validity at the time of attribution

While considering this (genuine) report it may be worth noting the inclusion of 'Moves towards a Middle East peace' as part of your criteria for analysis.

In the days before war broke out, war was not perceived as being part of a strategy for peace. Combat was regarded as anti-peace and 'Moves towards peace', at the time, were perceived to have failed. By the time the statement was printed an attitudinal change was taking place in the media and among politicians. The end of the war signalled that the conflict had been a necessary and important component of peace making.

At an earlier point in time, war might be given an adverse rating as a contribution towards peace, but after the shift in attitude had taken place war may have improved its rating to beneficial as a component of 'Moves towards Middle East peace and stability'. This raises a very important issue of attribution. The attribution is only valid when the circumstances are constant. In this case the difference of a few weeks changed the perception in the media and so attribution *at the same time* is critical in giving judgements of BNA.

Attributing to the writer

Attribution to the source of news is also covered in Chapter 4 in relation to the activities of a press office. But in all press coverage there is an intermediary. Journalists and editors have a significant say in what is published, so tracking the most important influences on a subject is significant. Look to attribute comment to an editor or journalist and note the name of the editor or, as is often the case, the reporter or correspondent. When a single by-line is used, this is complicated enough, but when more than one journalist contributes to a single article, the problem is compounded.

Journalists' attitudes

When tracking the attitudes of a single journalist, look for the occasions when his or her name coincides with a key word or issue. Over a relatively short period, a simple ranking of occurrences of a journalist's name against each key word will show reporting tendencies. Doing the same with multiple journalists covering the same key words or topics provides a similar listing but needs to be carried out over a longer period.

Certainly this kind of measure is important for planning campaigns where identifying journalists' attitudes is required. More advanced monitoring, which is especially valuable in the area of tracking attitudinal change, would consider all the different types of coverage.

In most journals there will be matter which is exclusively editorial. Much will be the work of two distinct types of journalist: reporters and correspondents. There will also be contributions from external sources, obvious examples being contributions to letters pages and exclusive articles from writers, such as press officers, whose work is published with little editing.

The type of correspondence will reflect the editorial stance of the publication. All papers have more copy than can possibly be published. As a result decisions on content are taken over a waste-paper bin. For the press analyst, attempting to sort out which material came from which source is complex. The letters column is quite straightforward though and will identify both the contributor and attitudinal changes on the part of the publication and among letter writers. The latter have considerable significance in their role as opinion formers.

CARMA: Computer Aided Research and Media Analysis

Moving into the realms of attribution and the movement of opinion among opinion formers, the work of A J Barr & Company, Washington and CARMA International Ltd, Surrey becomes quite fascinating. Designed to provide a service assisting with identification of trends and issues, the documentation of public opinion and a scientific basis on which to allocate resources for public relations, marketing and lobbying, these two organisations provide an interesting insight into the effectiveness of press relations monitoring.

The service they offer is called CARMA (Computer-Aided Research & Media Analysis). CARMA electronically sorts and analyses volumes of news generated by a variety of media and prepares results in a concise report. I am indebted to Sandra Macleod for the following contribution from CARMA studies.

Case studies: American Express and the EEC

Is the media projecting the right image and are companies managing the news and news makers as closely as they manage their strategic or marketing programmes? While many are not, some of the more sophisticated, large and small alike, are.

American Express, for instance, while running among the most professional in-house public relations teams was critical of the lack of professionalism and accountability of the PR and marketing function. In a feature article on CARMA, Germany's leading business publication, *Manager Magazine*, quotes Thomas Holtrop, former European Director of Public Affairs and Communications at AMEX: 'I know of several CEOs for different industries who all complain about the same deficiencies of their PR departments.'

As the article explains, PR professionals themselves often lament common problems.

- In contrast to their colleagues from the advertising or production division, the hands of PR managers are empty when it comes to justifying the value of their efforts to the Board when discussing budgets, 'data and facts are required because only numbers count when it comes to getting a fair share of the cake'.

- In-house PR teams consider themselves observers of all circumstances relevant to the company; however, there is often not enough time to follow closely the activities of the competition.
- International companies usually know exactly where they stand in their home markets, but not in markets abroad.

For these reasons, American Express turned to CARMA International with its seven-year track record for leading organisations in the United States. In conjunction with the in-house PR department at AMEX, the CARMA team developed the research guidelines for a detailed content analysis of the media's debate on the credit card market. The objectives were to determine American Express' image, to track changes in the market and to provide an early warning system for negative trends and influences initially in two countries: the UK and Spain.

In addition, Amex's senior management was demanding to be spared the unnerving flow of press articles into already overfull in-trays, and instead, wanted to be provided with concise, measurable and meaningful intelligence. As Holtrop said himself: 'In every large company, piles of newspaper articles, essays and the like are collected but nobody has time to tidy up the chaos and extract the results – least of all senior management.'

And yet it is precisely senior management who should be keeping their fingers on the pulse of the corporate image and competitive arena. What is the benefit of extensive in-house media relations and monitoring if this service lives in the dark without recognition or attention?

At this point, the CARMA team was called in to take over the 'brainwork' and analysis of those piles of cuttings with trained researchers to evaluate the raw material and produce graphs and charts to provide the in-house PR department with tangible results.

American Express was interested in corporate image, brand-specific attributes, industry issues and legislation. The CARMA research proved that one of the company's greatest problems was that the media (and ergo their clients) believed that the American Express card was expensive at a time when credit cards were starting to charge nominal amounts and expand their range of services accordingly – making inroads into Amex's traditional lead in customer benefits. American Express' PR managers reflected on the CARMA results to find better ways to communicate the card's perceived 'value for money'.

Amex was interested in brand specific issues and attributes – including 'global service'. The client wanted to prove to his colleagues, in a tangible way, and without depending on vague suppositions, how much importance the media – and indirectly AMEX clients – attributed to the universal acceptance of credit cards.

The CARMA team filtered a clear tendency out of the untidy pile of publications: 72 per cent of analysed articles rated world-wide global service as positive. By the same token, American Express was not recognised as a market leader in this area. 'A real number, at last', recalls Holtrop, 'We could build on it and, consequently, emphasise this aspect in all our campaigns.' Even notoriously critical colleagues were impressed by the stringent analysis of the researchers, and finally pulled their weight.

On another occasion, American Express needed to know which journalists and opinion formers had created a negative image for the company in a certain area in order to give them a tailored press briefing afterwards. The CARMA programme produced a comprehensive list of exactly who was sitting on which side of the fence and on which issues.

American Express in Spain had a very limited number of articles mentioning it by name in the Spanish media – about 50 clips on average – but even with these, a clear tendency for the national media to support AMEX's initiatives in the Spanish tourism industry vied against the local media's antagonism to the 'foreign American multinational'.

Holtrop commented: 'Quality was consistently given – simple content summaries would not have helped us. It was the analysis and recommendations, or the "food for thought", that we benefited from.' He went on to reflect that 'Without support, amateurs in communications can easily get themselves a bloody nose in this business.'

By using computer know-how CARMA was able to provide American Express with a host of information directly onto the client's computer. Once a journalist calls, by punching in a few keys on a desk terminal, the PR manager is able to call up the profile of the caller on the screen even before the preliminary chit-chat is over. Before him he can see how many stories the journalist has written about American Express or any of its competitors, how many were

Evaluating Press Coverage

negative, how many were unfair, and what issues he or she tends to write about. Amex also quickly learned the publication's editorial stance on the credit card debate and what the pattern of letters to its editor is (Figure 6.1).

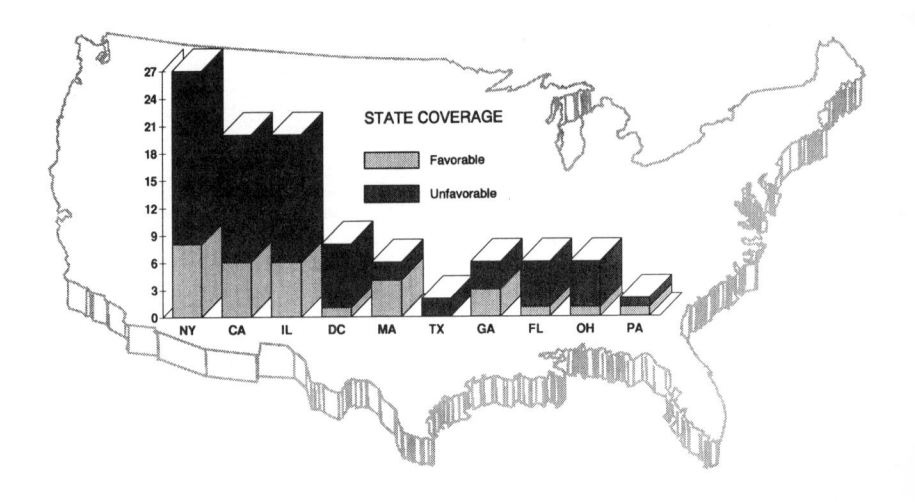

Figure 6.1 Issues tracking from coast to coast: CARMA gallops ahead . . .

Meanwhile, in the US, CARMA had been retained by the Delegation of the Commission of European Communities in Washington DC to track the great American public's attitudes to 1992. By examining some 910 articles in 1989, CARMA warned the Commission that the American public knew little about the EC, and most of what they were told by the media was negative. CARMA advised the

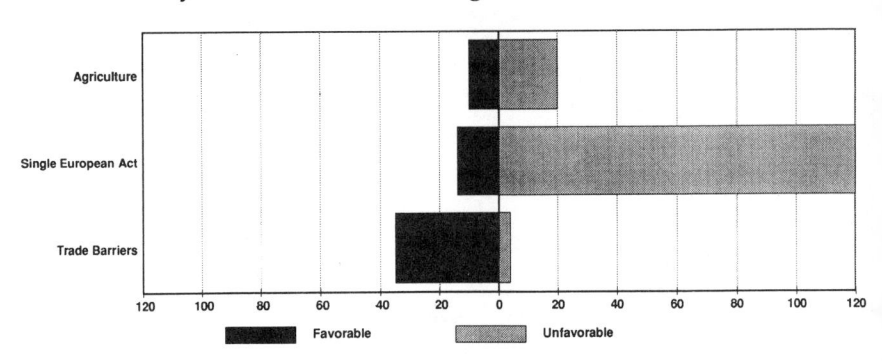

Figure 6.2 Attitudes in the USA to the European Single Market: leading favourable/unfavourable arguments

Attribution

Commission on which key messages about the unification of the single European market needed addressing in order to alter the public's largely negative perceptions (Figure 6.2).

Analysis showed that the overwhelmingly unfavourable argument carried by the media at that time was that the unification of Europe mounted to a 'fortress Europe' policy that would mean increased protectionism and would further divide the globe into regional trading blocks. Almost all sources at the time believed that US companies that were not already established in Europe by 1992 would effectively be shut out of the European market.

Possible impressions for this argument were 37.8 million readers. Furthermore CARMA revealed that opinion-moulding editorials were unfavourable by a 2:1 margin: almost all of them dealing with the 'fortress Europe' argument and the European ban on hormone-treated US beef (Figure 6.3).

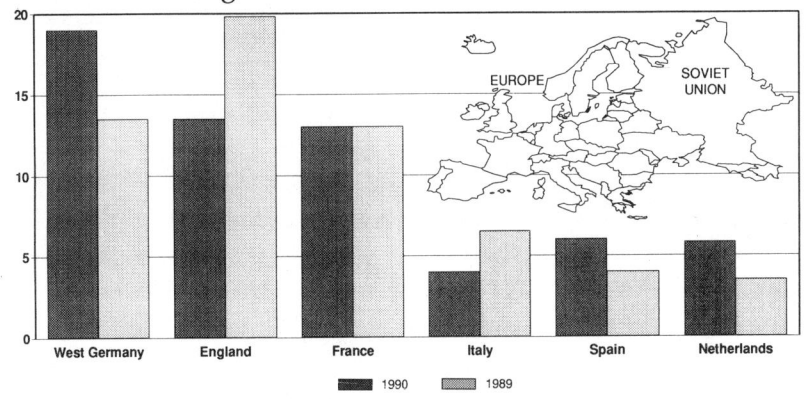

Figure 6.3 Leading coverage by country (% of total: 1989 vs 1990)

The issue was again revisited the following year. This time, Gallup was commissioned to undertake a similar study based on focused telephone interviews of 1001 adults nationwide during February and March.

Within a few weeks in early April 1990, based on another 1000 articles in the first quarter of 1990, CARMA reported that Americans were beginning to see enormous potential in a unified EC while fears of a 'fortress Europe' were beginning to subside. Favourable coverage was up by 50 per cent, news pieces and editorials had increased their favourability ratio by 50 per cent. The fall of Communist regimes in Eastern Europe and the possibility of a unified Germany raised the possibility of a greatly expanded

Evaluating Press Coverage

market, one in which it will be increasingly difficult to keep outsiders away. In the media coverage, many US companies now see a much improved potential for new European marketing.

In 1989, CARMA found that media coverage was mainly concerned with protectionist trends in the EC. However, in 1990, the change in issue coverage is noteworthy, although due largely to political upheaval, and suggestive of a shift in US opinion toward the EC. It also indicates favourable moves toward investment in a newly expanded Eastern European market had begun. Of note was that less coverage on controversial agricultural issues in 1990 contributed to an improvement in the reporting (Figure 6.4).

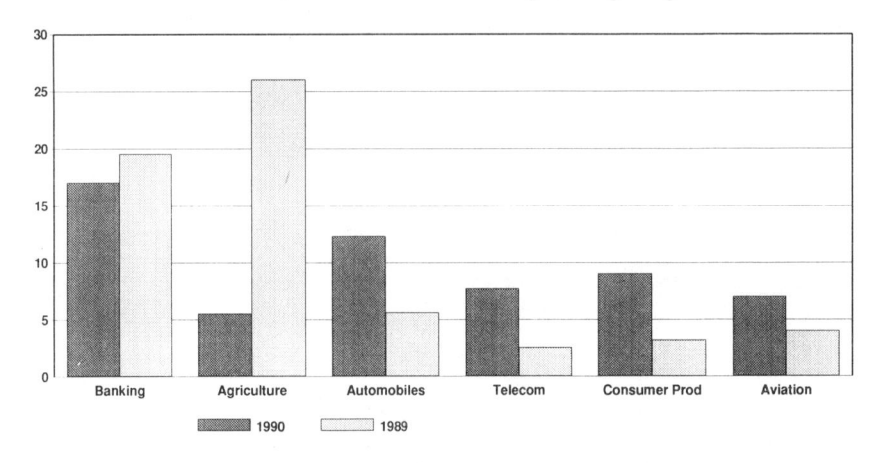

Figure 6.4 Leading sectoral issues (% of total: 1989 vs 1990)

This content analysis clearly showed that while some Americans were uncertain about the business and political ramifications of an integrated European market, 'EC 1992' was taking on new meaning for all Americans who are beginning to understand the importance of the concept of a global marketplace.

In addition, CARMA reported on the changes in patterns of coverage, regional reach, trends and sources of news. For instance, in 1989, the leading unfavourable source of news was none other than Margaret Thatcher by a long margin (Figure 6.5).

In 1990, she remained the most outspoken critic to appear in the US media. She gave no support to the Social Charter concepts, as did her counterparts Helmut Kohl and Francois Mitterand. US Trade Representative Carla Hills appeared often in the media on trade reciprocity concerns in 1990, and on her opposition to the directive on television broadcasting in 1989. Interestingly, CARMA found

Attribution

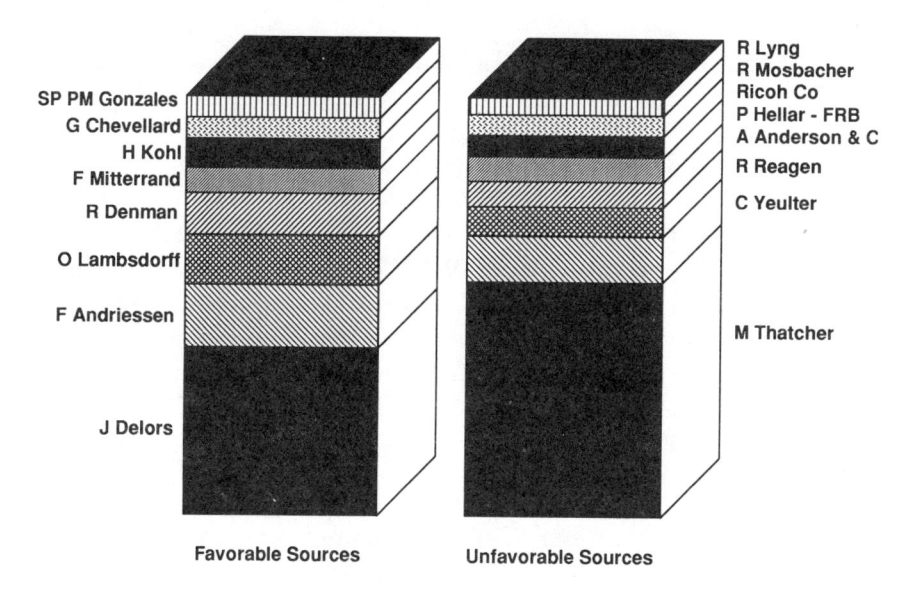

Figure 6.5 Leading sources of news: 1989

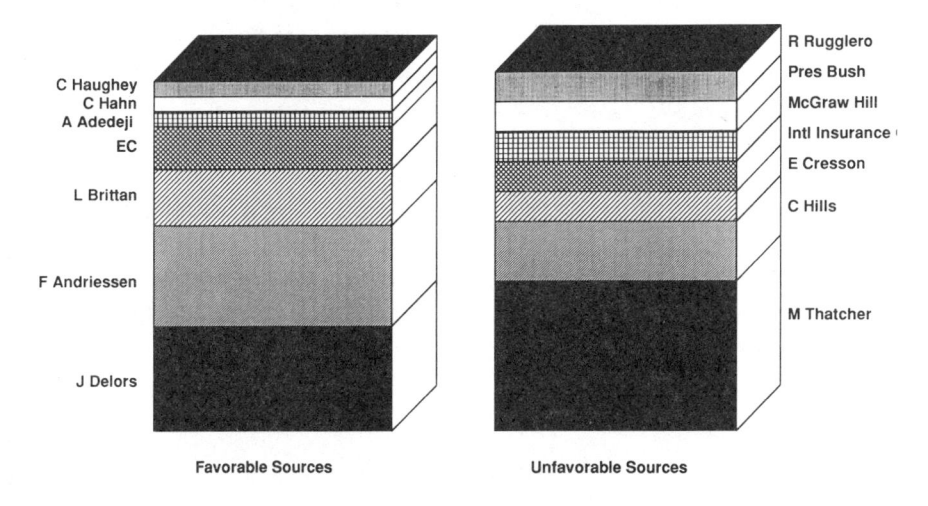

Figure 6.6 Leading sources of news: January–March 1990

that she was not retaliating against the EC concerning telecommunications during 1990 (Figure 6.6).

By way of supportive comparison, Gallup announced its survey results on 17 May. Headlines ran: 'New Poll Finds Americans Positive on Europe and 1992'. Gallup revealed that:

> Forty-seven per cent of all American adults say that they have 'heard or read about' the European Community ... This dramatic change from the level encountered in 1987 when a previous poll found only 20 per cent of the population to be familiar with the EC. Those who are aware of the single market are more likely to see it as good (50 per cent) rather than bad (17 per cent) for American consumers. Seventy-five percent of the total sample believes that the US should develop a 'special relationship' with the European Community as a whole. Again, among those familiar with the EC, the rating was even higher (82 per cent).

The above not only gives credence to the rule that 'familiarity and favourability' are closely linked, but also proves how effective media content analysis can be in predicting public attitudes and opinions.

Putting aside the cost of commissioning original research from polling organisations, media content analysis tracks the evolution of issues and favourability on a day-in-day-out basis. Constantly. Objectively. Thoroughly. Accurately.

Thanks to the power of the computer, the concept of media content analysis has come of age. Such analysis provides a regular measurement of how reputation is shifting. Why it is shifting ? And what can be done about it?

Organisations from Sony in Tokyo, through to American Express and The European Commission have all learned to benefit by keeping one step ahead in their strategic communications with both the makers and the purveyors of news.

Audience perception

There are two distinct types of attribution: the perception directly attributable to the subject under scrutiny and the perception of the audience. But attribution has its difficulties, as the following example may help illustrate:

If the key word is dog (ie we take a dog's view of the article), then in 'man bites dog', the comment is adverse for dog. In 'dog bites man' the attribution is beneficial to dog. A different readership, would have 'man' as the audience. Now man may have a different view and a different attribution could be given. If, however, 'dog's'

Attribution

PR campaign is trying to clean up dog's image as maneater, then the coverage is adverse.

Further analysis of the audience shows that being complex, man might be anti-dog and when 'man bites dog', will be supportive of man. Some men, however, might believe the action cruel to dog and sympathise with him.

Audience perception is all-important.

Direct attribution to key word

Maintaining key word or key issue as the basis for the analysis, the judgement least open to interpretation is to view the key word and such commentary which can be directly attributed to it. If the comment can be described as beneficial, neutral or adverse, that attribution should be given regardless of other comment which in context may give a different impression.

A friend with a passion for collecting stamps was quoted in a national newspaper as saying 'I once bought my wife a rare stamp for her birthday. She was furious!' The name of his company, of which he was chairman, was prominent in the article.

The friend was a 'key word'. We all enjoyed the joke. He was furious as this snippet was repeated in umpteen newspapers and gossip columns and was somewhat embarrassed at the indiscretion. His wife was cross at being quoted in the 'rags'. Was this beneficial, neutral or adverse?

One may imagine there is almost no one who would not see the funny side of the anecdote and in terms of showing a human side to the friend, it certainly did little harm and the added publicity for the company has some value.

The media analyst sided with the friend because the attributed coverage was 'adverse' to the key word but gave a 'neutral' rating to the company, being neither beneficial nor adverse.

Had the audience been tightly specified, the result may have been different. A definition of audience such as 'union official' could have been adverse on the presumed grounds that the gift was frivolous and demonstrated self interest. Alternatively an audience which included 'wife's bank manager' may have been 'beneficial' as the friend was improving the assets of the customer.

Subjective or objective

Press analysis for BNA has to take into account the different approaches. If a system does not include an element of audience perception (a subjective method), an assessment between a company and its competitors can look distorted. For example a beneficial comment for a competitor could be construed as being adverse to the company.

To provide an even more startling example imagine the case of assessing coverage about Saddam Hussein as he puts down a revolt in his country! For reports saying he is 'succeeding' in his endeavour, attribution will be beneficial, however distasteful to the analyst. However a simple word added, such as 'cruelly succeeding. . . .' will change the attribute to adverse.

Nevertheless, this method of attributing BNA is valid and as long as it is constant, interpretation will not be complicated.

Audience briefing

For most campaigns identifying audience is not so critical that fine judgements are needed but for most major organisations audience specification and a brief on how to interpret coverage are necessary.

In such circumstances the brief will need a number of elements. A well defined audience will include an attitude interpretation (preferably well researched) as part of the description. Such a brief may say that the audience is:

- well disposed;
- critically well disposed;
- critically ill disposed;
- ill disposed to the key word;

or

- benignly competitive;
- aggressively competitive.

Some further judgements can be added to describe the relationship of the audience; such a brief enables correct attribution of value.

Context

The measure does not stop at audience identification; there is also a question of context. If all competitors are getting panned and the client is not, is the client likely to be tarred with the same brush? What difference does it make if:

1 The client is not included?
2 The client is included in a neutral/favourable light?

When reading the article, with an audience brief, a valid judgement can be made. In the strictest sense such measures have to apply to each element of the story, eg headline, copy and photograph. How to attribute these measures in a form which is going both to report fact and provide valuable research for future campaign planning is now very important.

If the measure is to be simplistic and not take the audience analyst into account, every small snippet of coverage can be given a prominence rating such as ccm. In such instances there will be absolute numbers to provide the guidelines and future tracking will show the effect of campaigning.

Independent research for perceptions

Conversely, a comprehensive analysis of audience, audience perceptions and attitudes, will provide a report on the probable effect of coverage and can be compared with other research to track probable attitudinal change and campaign effectiveness.

This is a specialist form of analysis and should be left to experts. At the end of the day interpretation will need trained assessors and constancy in measurement will require comparative testing between analysts, against researched perceptions and each other (inter-rater reliability) to ensure valid attribution is made consistently. Social scientists and opinion pollsters have considerable experience in this field and an appreciable amount of testing for advertising campaigns has used this type of technique. There is no doubt that such research is valuable and it will become even more important in the future as public relations moves towards targeting behaviourial change.

Forecasting attitudes to coverage

With opinion research running in parallel there is every opportunity to gain some idea of probable attitudinal change and, with fast analysis, there is the possibility that having such measures available it will be possible to identify campaign changes needed between, say, the time newspapers are printed and read.

For more purist research, the closer you get to absolutes, the better the result. A case where a key phrase or word is repeated can be measured in terms of number of appearances, number of different contexts and number of different publications. The next stage, which looks at the make up of the circulation and household penetration, probability of being read and by whom, begins to add many new dimensions to the assessment. If an attempt is then made to establish how the message is interpreted by the readers the number of variables increases.

Each dimension has to be given an attribution which has to take into account probability as well as known and indisputable factors. As the number of different aspects of the influence of an article is increased so too are the opportunities for discretion and inaccuracy in attribution by the assessor. The need to find an optimum number of different measures to include is critical. Some content analysis reports are so full of statistics that only the brave will attempt to interpret them. With computers running sophisticated mathematical programmes, comparative models can be prepared. Thus a particular range of content-analysis attributes can be compared to past experience which has been confirmed through independent research and the *likelihood* of a message delivery can then be predicted with some confidence.

With highly trained analysts, the attribution should be quite good, although there is too little research available yet to pass judgement.

On turning to the identification of the entry of issues into the media and change in the relative forcefulness of issues, a different type of assessment is required. Here the measure may not be one of 'beneficial, neutral and adverse' but instead may be measured in terms of acceptance, contribution, ambivalence, detraction and rejection.

In many ways public relations is concerned more with issues than products, people and institutions. To change opinion, issues have to be thought of as propositions (environmental pollution may be an issue but the proposition is that pollution is bad). Identifying products, people and institutions with a proposition in mind can be difficult for the public relations practitioner more used to product marketing PR as part of promotion.

To identify the work of a journalist writing about a product within the context of a proposition we need to view the coverage as:

- engendering acceptance;
- contributing to success or development;
- ambivalent;
- detracting from;
- rejecting.

To measure all coverage about a product in such terms will quickly identify the kind of press relations job that needs to be done and the kind of relationship one audience, the journalist, has with the product or product concept.

An influencing medium

Here the press is not treated as a selling medium but as an influencing medium, a role where it is both effective and comfortable.

The ability to analyse this type of coverage in this way is available but it is more costly because it requires both better trained analysis and longer to unravel the data. Presentation of the findings is simple and is easy for a public relations specialist to interpret. The experience of people who have made the effort to use this kind of analysis has made them very committed to the concept but selling the idea to industrial, commercial and marketing managers is a different story. The up-front benefit is poorly understood and simpler methods are more likely to prevail in the short term.

Campaigning

Having looked at coverage in absolute terms there is an attribution of value based on whether the article was effective in promoting campaign objectives. It is in the field of campaigning, as opposed to message carrying (marketing promotion) that types of measurement from an audience's perception are most effective.

Evaluating Press Coverage

Going back to the 'dog bites man' illustration, assuming that everyone believes dogs bite man, analysis of coverage for dog could include an audience defined as 'man' with a prejudice 'against dog' based on fear and pain having been regularly bitten.

Dog may campaign on a variety of propositions such as 'dog does not want to bite man'. Measurement for tracking attitudinal change will centre on coverage providing:

- acceptance;

- contribution to dog's proposition;

- ambivalence;

- dog proposition detractors;

- dog proposition rejection.

On the other hand a measure of the media view of 'dog' will be to look at 'dog' as a key word and attribute measures of beneficial, neutral, adverse. This will not directly measure campaign effectiveness but will tell us if the dog image is changing among journalists.

Here we see a dog story with great potential and its effectiveness will be in the pervasive nature of the campaigns. Opportunities to see, unprompted coverage (eg taken from other journals) and the willingness to accept press release material are all good measures of campaign effectiveness and the impact of the story on the page.

However, it is important to watch other issues and simultaneously to track the proportion of, and total coverage available, to the subject/campaign. Monitoring other issues can dramatically change a press relations campaign as in the case of the bull.

When 'Bull gores man', a dog bite seems quite tame! However, to be sure, independently researched audience perceptions of dog bites man and bull gores man could be undertaken to confirm that the latter really is more horrifying. If it is proven to be so, then attribution can be confident but, without independent and parallel research such attribution will be, to some extent, subject to a caveat.

During the Gulf War, Iraq and the conflict pushed all other issues aside. In the USA, eleven national journals dropped coverage of all other issues for the duration.

Attribution

Measuring attitudes to plan campaigns

A more down-to-earth application of these arguments can be found in everyday press campaigns.

If we look at, for example, the relative importance of issues for motor car manufacturers, tracking may well provide the clue as to which feature to promote to achieve the most favourable coverage. Imagine selecting issues such as:

- performance;
- safety;
- fire hazard.

It is reasonable to look at press coverage and find out what the media regards as the proposition surrounding these areas of interest in motor cars. There may be a proposition which identifies 'performance' as a wholly good thing and so the proposition will be that 'performance' predominantly will get good press. On the other hand there may be a predisposition among journalists that cars are not very 'safe'. This may not always be coincidental with the proposition that 'performance' is inter alia bad but there could be an overlapping relationship to the two issues and the two propositions. In such a case 'safe performance' may be a much more effective proposition for the press officer to promote to the media than either 'performance' or 'safety'. If 'fire hazard' appears as a stand-alone issue, it may be that fire retardation features in a car will give the manufacturer a significant edge over competitors. Issues provide potent coverage and once tracked provide essential information for the press relations planner.

Putting a qualitative judgement on articles is not a precise science and there are any number of ways to examine the problem. It can be done and, for the most part, well-considered methods in use are very valuable. In time they will become critical to every campaign.

Lack of understanding of this area of press relations on the part of either client or consultant will, in the next few years, lead to tears. The effectiveness of consultants with the necessary skills will be well in advanced of the erstwhile 'press release writer' and press campaigns have the potential to be ever more effective.

Language and reading skills

The mainstay of journalism and public relations is communication. For the most part different languages are used for different audiences. Knowing how effectively meaning can be distinguished by using slang and acronyms is part of realising how good people are as communicators.

Take the expression 'collateral damage', which is a military euphemism for enemy civilian casualties, interpreting the effect of such a phrase will be difficult but not impossible. As most people do not know what such a phrase means, the full horror of the event will escape them. Identifying experimentally audience understanding of press coverage, including jargon, using well known audience research methods can be done. This is fine in the case stated above. If, however, the situation is being judged in, say an industrial context, with competitors using a variety of different expressions and acronyms to describe products, the issues and measurements can be blurred.

For example: If readers do not have a good or perfect understanding of what 'DOS' is, 'DOS compatible' is meaningless. For many, the full name 'disk operating system' may not be sufficient and the lengthier 'computer disk operating system' may be needed before a particular audience has sufficient knowledge base to come to a conclusion. What perception such an audience has of a particular article or series of articles is heavily dependent on both reading skills and the different languages used in the press.

As monitoring coverage becomes more usual, audience perception and understanding will need further research to gain valid impressions of the effect of press coverage.

7

The Competition as a Yardstick

Progressively, competitors have been introduced into the measurement equation. The reasons are relatively simple but must be understood. There are very few absolutes that can be used when looking at cuttings. Comparing how effective a client is against competition provides an excellent measure (Figure 7.1). Fair warning, it is wise to be a little wary before completely believing this statement.

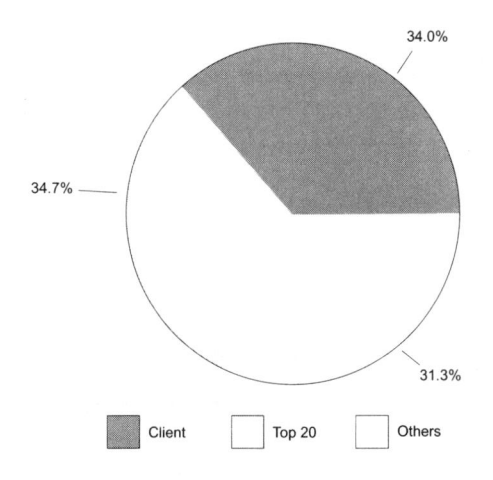

Figure 7.1 Industry coverage in ccm of top 20/client/others

As long as a reader's regard for the content of a publication over time is unchanging, coverage which provides a direct comparison between two organisations is very helpful. Regrettably though, stability of readers' perceptions of journals fluctuates.

At one particular time television may be more believable than newspapers, but later these ratings may be reversed. Some publications become fashionable while others' circulations decline. The very source material you are using as the basis for your research (the press) is a moving entity.

If you cannot measure what publications represent in terms of stability among readers, a comparison of coverage about any particular subject in the same publications over a six month period may not be valid. If attitudes towards a publication change – and they do – so too do attitudes towards products and issues.

As we have seen, we need to be able to base assessment in real time so that we measure coverage when reader perceptions are the same and this means we need a real time yardstick (see Chapter 6).

Compare the similar in nature

The best yardstick is an akin entity which is affected by the vagaries of press popularity in the same way and to the same extent. This base, from which you can draw acceptable conclusions, will need to have the same or similar impact on the audience which you are trying to motivate.

One of the best yardsticks is competitor operation in very closely related circumstances. This provides an effective answer to the problem of measuring press reaction in real time and over a prolonged period. Simply, competitors operating in the same environment should, all other factors being equal, attain the same relative performance over any given period.

There are problems, of course. One competitor may become more active or may respond to a campaign better than others, or be subject to other influences which change its profile. To overcome such problems we look to a larger universe, perhaps the client 'sector' or 'industry'. This could include all competitors or a selection most closely related to the client. While there may be changes in one or two competitors, the relative change will be less pronounced and will assist in validating our research.

The Competition as a Yardstick

Competitors and issues

By using the term competitor, one tends to ignore other comparable measures. To measure the effectiveness of the press work of political parties it is easy to transfer from the concept of commercial enterprises but what of measuring the effectiveness of a corporate or financial campaign. In such instances the competitive measure may well be in a different kind of enterprise altogether.

The same goes for tracking issues. There will always be issues competing for attention and changes in attitudes which can be called 'akin' are assessed in the same way.

How then to identify 'competitors' to provide the basis for comparison: the secret is to find the audience with an 'akin' interest. Commercially this will often simply be customers or consumers. Furthermore, for a company selling a product, the competitors providing the yardstick will be those organisations with a competing product.

The audience

If, on the other hand, one is tracking an issue, its relative importance may be compared to another issue which also affects the same people to a comparable degree. The importance of unemployment as an issue may be associated with income support payments and housing benefits. The audience is largely the same and the prospects of employment and social payments to the unemployed will be closely related issues.

Multiple issues

There is, of course, no reason why only one issue should be tracked at one time. The benefit of tracking multiple issues is that the universe is extended and the importance rating of the principal key issue against a basket of other (notable and akin) issues will be in relation to a wider universe of opinion. A more valid sample.

As for companies – so for politicians. Here the objective may be to change the view of electors or opinion formers but when it comes to issues, selecting the 'customer' can be much more profound. We will concentrate on commercial usage but it is translatable and experience is growing all the time.

The principles of measurement remain the same as for measuring home-grown press relations output. The luxury of knowing competitors' press release output would be useful but the detective work is not practical even though some stories can be tracked and coverage for specific stories (such as new product launches) is easily identified.

How many competitors to track

Tracking competitor coverage need not encompass all; a selected top three, five or such number is adequate. The largest number known to be tracked consistently is twenty, with the rest included in a category called 'others' (this latter section has its own quarterly programme to identify an emergent player, if any, in the media).

The concept of comparing competitive coverage to validate press relations effectiveness also allows a client to review the working of a press office in direct relationship with competing press offices. Competitors, and coverage of individual competing products, will show similar profiles as for the home-grown press relations campaigns. There is an added benefit in that the universe is greater, and therefore even more accurate and valid. Measures and assessment techniques are already well described.

Information available from competitive analysis

Comparative analysis will provide confirmation of style and content. If the need for feature length material, case studies and photographs is high it will have an influence on programme planning, content and cost.

Historical analysis

One of the joys of press coverage analysis is that it can be historical, providing a retrospective view of all the coverage and activities of competitors over a prior month, three months or even three years – a task which is no more difficult than finding the cuttings. This research is invaluable when planning press relations programmes.

The Competition as a Yardstick

The life of a story

Additionally, the life of a story (such as a new product release) in individual journals will be important for the various phases of a marketing plan (Figure 7.2). An examination of the growth of coverage to its peak provides the marketing manager with the means to time press campaigns into promotional campaigns very precisely. In addition, a review of competing PR budgeted expenditure is possible and resources can be effectively allocated.

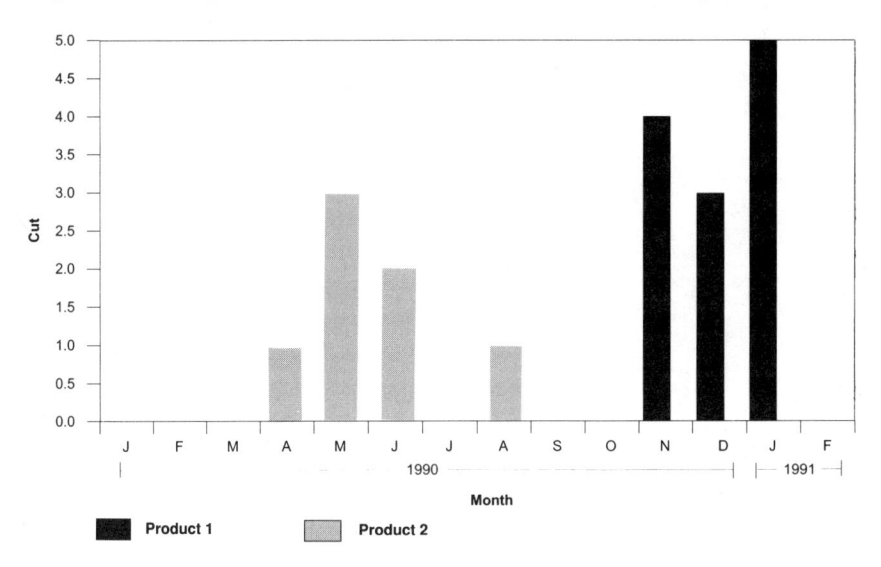

Figure 7.2 Press coverage in 1990: selected releases/products appearances

Acceptability of different stories

It is interesting to discover how much is reported about an industry or product (Figure 7.3). Data can cover the number of articles (Figure 7.4), their exclusivity and total and average lengths, photographs used and the peaks and troughs in coverage during the year. For many programmes, sure knowledge about the need for (and type of) photographs required could save sufficient enough budget to more than pay for the whole of this measurement and evaluation activity; for some, savings will be out of all proportion.

The spread of journals reporting competitor products not only assists in refining press lists but also shows where niche coverage has been historically practical.

Evaluating Press Coverage

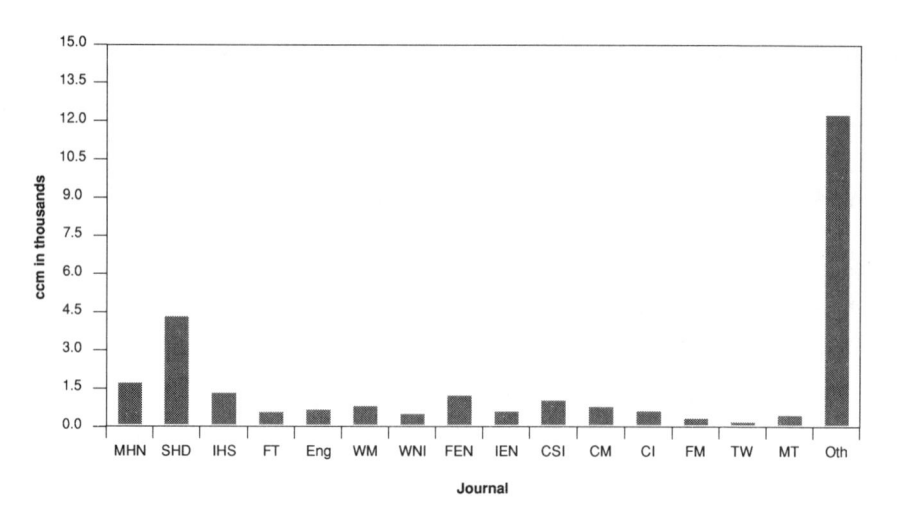

Figure 7.3 Industry coverage in ccm in selected journals 1990

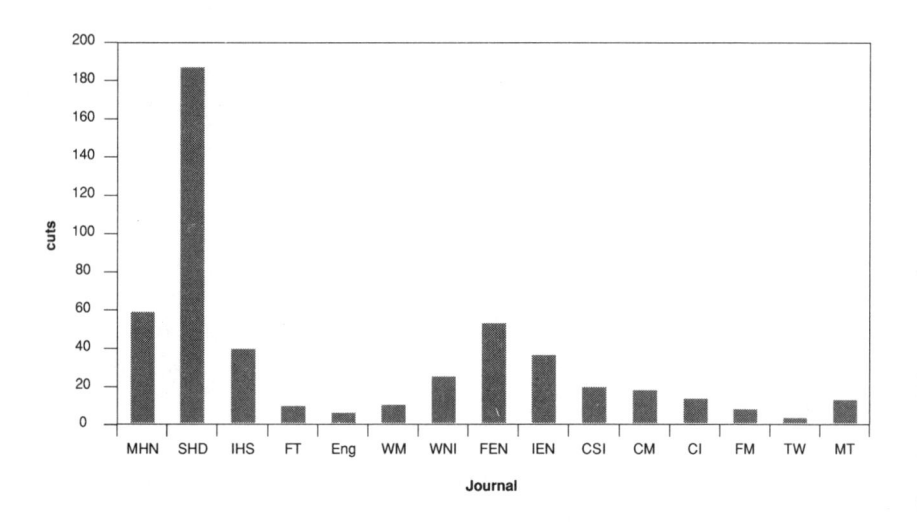

Figure 7.4 Industry coverage: appearances in selected journals 1990

Relative measurement between different companies or product coverage also provides insight into how much effort is required to provide comparable or better coverage (see Figure 7.3) and, where market data is available, the movement of coverage compared to market share can be assessed if 'noise' by way of other promotional effort can be filtered out of the calculation.

The Competition as a Yardstick

The value of this information, not only for campaign planning and budgeting, but in assessing effectiveness, cannot be overstated. For the marketeer and the press relations planner, the ability to use this data is invaluable. With more elements in the programme, corporate image assessment and shifts in potential to change perceptions can be tracked with accuracy. Strategic decisions with tactical capability can be included.

Resource monitor

With immediate effect, the press officer knows broadly how effective the programme is and the relative value of writers in competition with others in the same line. Over or underspend on press relations can be judged and, with good hard facts, budget adjustment is not only possible but mandatory. Wasted effort can be quickly eliminated and resources applied to areas of greatest need to maintain effective press presence.

While the amount of data collected and the time taken doing it is very low, the impact on campaign planning, budget and resource allocation is immeasurably enhanced.

On a regular basis the press officer should now be able to report effectiveness in the terms shown in Figure 7.5.

In a matter of a few weeks cumulative information can be charted in real numbers and graphically presented to provide invaluable data about both effectiveness and future need. This will show which journals report the company (or organisation) and its competitors. Such confirmation of the value of differing journals to a campaign is based on both the press office view as well as the cumulative (competing) press offices across an industry. No relevant journal will now be missed and those publications which, on the face of it, appear relevant but do not use press office output can be investigated with a view to their removal from press lists.

Relative strength of press offices

The relative strength of different press offices with particular publications will also be evident. From such information, effort to appeal to different journalists can be directed to improve penetration in the journals. Indeed, such data may even identify

Evaluating Press Coverage

those publications influenced by other factors such as competitor pressures.

Your Company Ltd
Executive Summary

01/04/91 11:11   Page I

Report 11. Period of this report 01/03/91 to 31/03/91

	PKW	ONW	Other	TOTAL	PKW % Of TOTAL
1 - BASE FOR ANALYSIS					
Total Journals	39	15	28	82	47
Total Articles	74	50	131	255	29
Available Editorial Measured (ccm)				8036	
2 - OVERVIEW					
Keyword ccm	1259	1450	3455	6164	20
Keyword	20	24	56	100	
3 - IMPACT					
Total Mentions on front pages	0				
Total Exclusive Cuttings	52	48	130	230	22
Exclusive Cuttings >=50 ccm	5	9	14	28	17
Exclusive Cuttings >=25<50 ccm	10	12	23	45	22
Exclusive Cuttings <25 ccm	37	27	93	157	23
Total Headlines	19	11	N/A	30	63
Photographs	29	42	65	136	21
4 - QUALITY					
Total Beneficial Mentions	65	77	N/A	142	45
Total Neutral Mentions	0	0	N/A	0	0
Total Adverse Mentions	9	0	N/A	9	100
5 - OPPORTUNITY TO ENQUIRE (ALL COVERAGE)					
Total Circulation ('000)	7669				
Contact Address included	48				
Telephone Numbers provided	65				
Reader Enquiry Number included	175				
Enquiry Coupon included	0				

Figure 7.5 Industry coverage: appearance of top 20 companies and others 1990

The Competition as a Yardstick

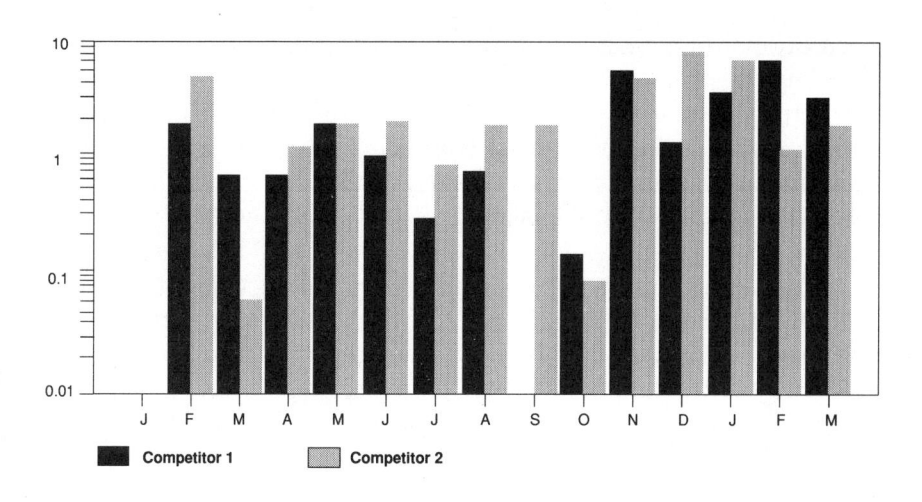

Figure 7.6 Average articles per press release

Source identification

People close to the media, such as company and competitor spokespeople, specialist journalists or academics will become evident, and useful information about where to invest in sending photographs will be important.

Progressive reports presented numerically or, better still, graphically also provide good information. Comparisons between the number of press releases issued and the resultant coverage and quality of coverage will emerge (Figure 7.6). Relative success between press offices will be evident and can be used to set targets as well as to measure effectiveness. Both absolute and proportional length of cuttings will provide quality quotients compared between press officers.

For sheer quality, the number of beneficial, exclusive and long articles with names in headlines and a photograph in key journals will start to become the pinnacle objective for press officers and an increasingly important part of future long-term planning.

If we take the point that issues can change (for example moves for peace in the Middle East) it is important to watch for changes in perceptions about products. Issues and product measurements are indivisible when it comes to monitoring. The USP of a product may become 'me too' and the features which were originally of great promotional benefit to the product can rapidly be interpreted as showing the product as out of date and to be avoided.

It is important to maintain tracking and to be alert to measures of beneficial, neutral and adverse. However, neutral is not the kind of material publications want or choose to publish. People do not read it but it often comes about as journalists change loyalty. Typically a neutral report is analogous to a voter abstaining; it reflects a change in stance. Neutral reports appear sparingly but are a very important marker and never to be ignored. Neutral heralds change and are fleeting.

A complete change in attitude in the press, say a move to supporting a single competitor, isolates a very forceful, highly motivated change in behaviour.

8
Tracking Press Coverage

When the press cuttings arrive you make an instant judgement on how well you have done. Add two words 'this month' and the beginning of tracking is already present. Not a few client meetings will follow on with the comment '.... and how will we do next month?' To answer that question without some idea of what has gone before is, at best, guess work. What you can track and the benefits of accumulating useable and useful data have been touched on already. There is much more. Setting parameters for tracking will depend on what the consultancy and client want to discover.

Deciding on timescale

While most tracking will be based on a timescale, dividing statistics into different time periods will be carefully considered and has to be dealt with elsewhere. For the time being consider the information accumulated at monthly intervals.

The chart in Figure 8.1 shows the level of output of material from a press office over a three-year period. This record of press releases issued is compiled from releases of original material and material issued from existing stocks of press releases reworked to meet the needs of editorial features.

You can see how the campaign developed and how strategic and budgetary decisions affected output, resulting in an overall picture.

Evaluating Press Coverage

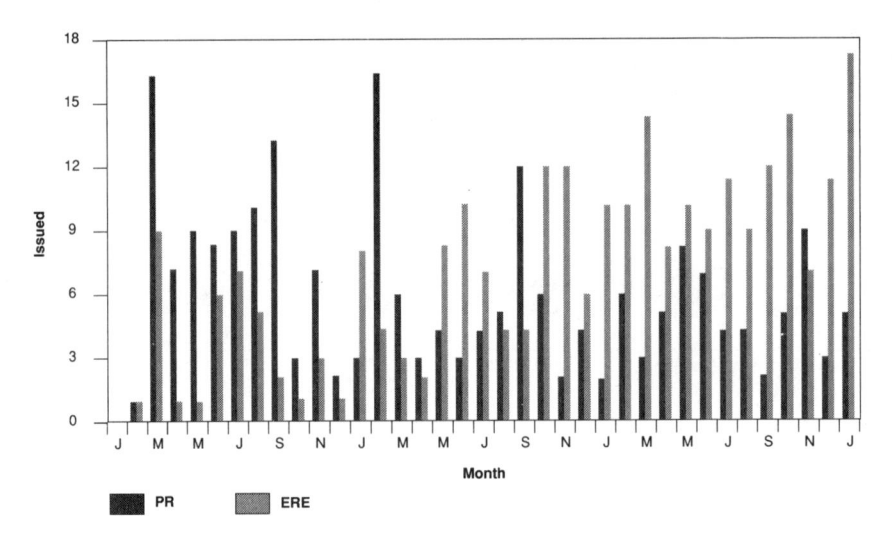

Figure 8.1 Press releases issued to the end of January 1991

Number of articles attributable

The most elementary record of effectiveness will be of the number of cuttings attributable to the client. A typical representation is given in Figure 8.2 and related directly to the output in Figure 8.1.

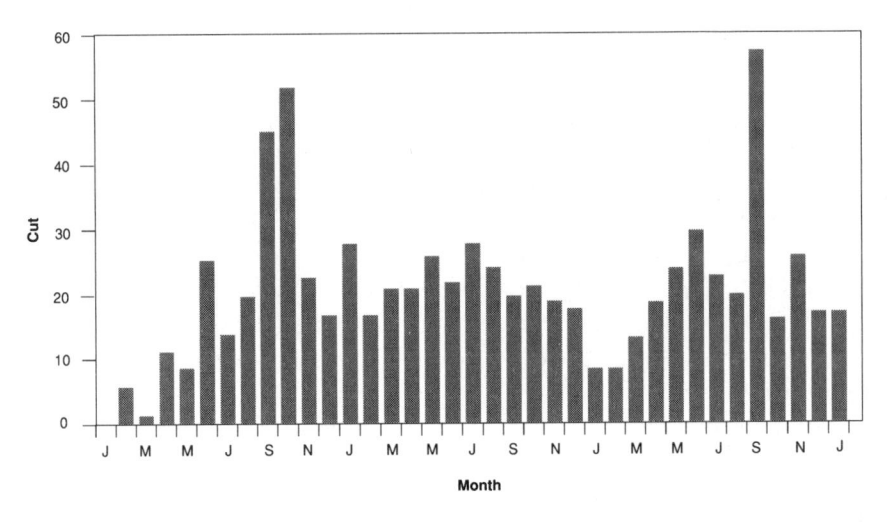

Figure 8.2 Articles published to the end of January 1991

Tracking Press Coverage

Visibility cycles

Here we can see client cuttings received over a three-year period. The underlying cycle becomes apparent after the third year with a fall-off at each year end. We can also see the effect of major events which provide peaks of coverage and the effect of reducing or increasing output of releases.

Managing coverage

This kind of tracking helps manage the account with client and consultancy identifying the effort made and to what effect.

There is every incentive for the consultancy to deliver and a powerful reason for the client to assist in providing story leads and to clear press releases for issue. This one measure encourages both parties to put a lot of material in the system to ensure that coverage is maintained.

Against this measure we can make some qualitative judgements by including a record of the number of column centimetres achieved (Figure 8.3).

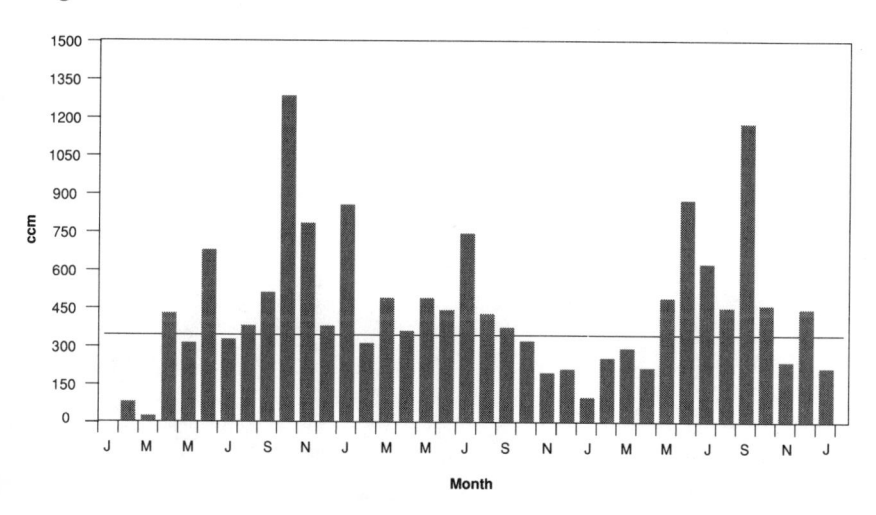

Figure 8.3 Column centimetres published to the end of January 1991

Evaluating Press Coverage

Variation between measures

For the uninitiated it is surprising to note how the relationship between cuttings and ccm does not follow as closely as one would imagine (Figure 8.4). Indeed, by measuring the average ccm against articles, the monthly fluctuation is quite marked (Figure 8.5).

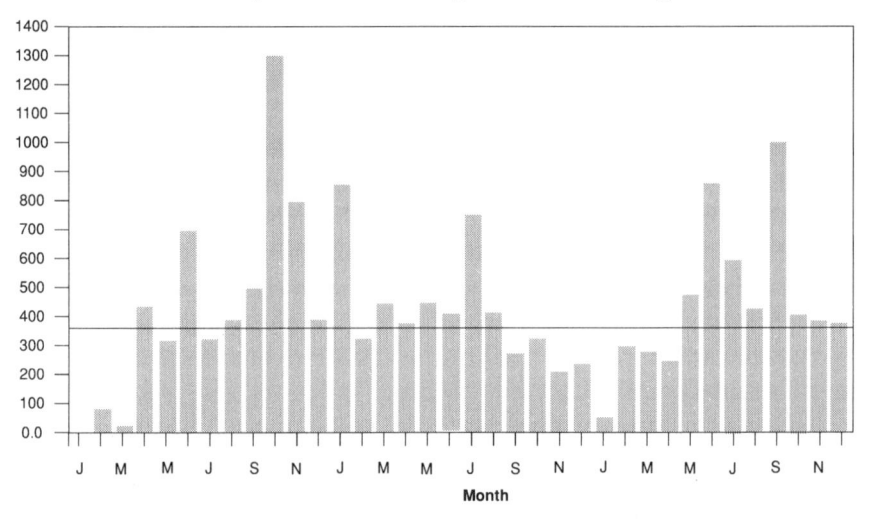

Figure 8.4 Client A: ccms published over a three-year period

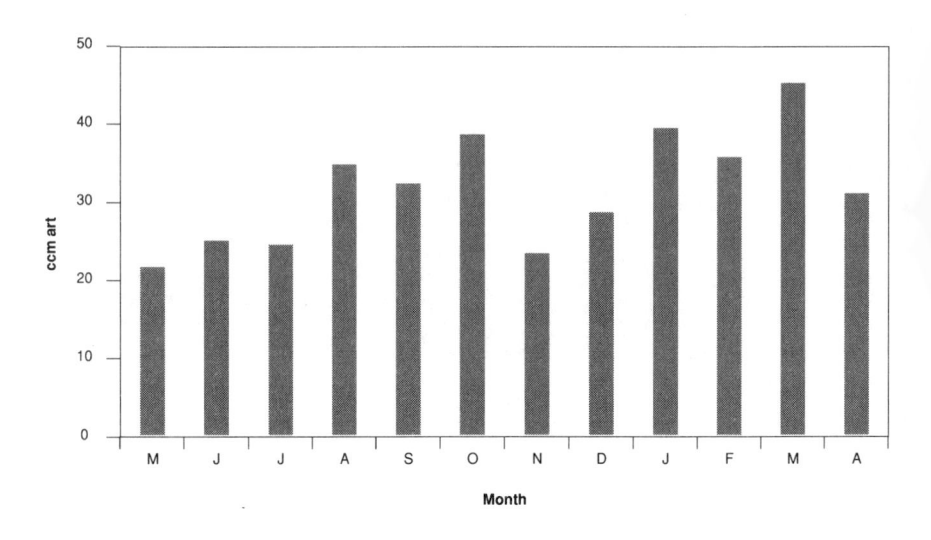

Figure 8.5 Company B: ccm per article

This allows the account executive to look back for a reason, draw conclusions about the circulation, type and quality of press releases issued and propose relevant action.

Monitor variance

Here it is important to identify what you are really doing. You are looking at the variation in coverage and the type of coverage. Tracking, above everything else, allows you to identify variance. Once identified, a review and remedial action can be implemented as and if necessary.

By keeping a record of dates issued and the time between release and peak coverage, you can identify the 'life' of a story.

Timing

A new product story, effectively targeted and timed, will give a campaign punch and presence at the appropriate time. Assume that you have 12 months' good statistics available. From this data it is possible to identify new product launch campaigns and the period taken to reach peak coverage and fall off (see Figure 7.2). Story lead times are now available for press stories in the national, consumer and trade media.

Additionally the lead time for order announcements, technical features, case studies and so on is identified, together with their acceptability in different journals. By back tracking, data on all journals available for coverage about the industry over the last year is available.

While the absolute control of timing and message achieved through advertising is very precise, planning press coverage timing is not an absolute science but with good records a great degree of certainty will be an invaluable weapon in the marketeer's armoury.

All too often public relations consultants and managers plead for and fail to get the appropriate time to achieve coincidental coverage for campaigns. A simple chart at the planning meeting will save all the argument. A track record over a number of campaigns is invaluable.

Monitoring peaks and troughs

The implications of this monitoring are far reaching. All subjects and products have a minimum core of dedicated coverage in any period of time. There is usually a short run up, a peak of coverage and then a period when the story tails off among publications. The period for peak visibility is a core period in the campaign. This core coverage will fluctuate for a variety of reasons and so it is important to look at what this core of exposure will be.

Taking the example of coverage available for all the political parties it is reasonable to assume a level of core coverage. There will be annual peaks at times of local elections and, rather like the run up to the State of the Union address in the USA, the UK has its run up over the weeks before and after the budget. There is also less coverage in normal circumstances during a parliamentary recess and a peak during a general election.

By tracking these trends it will soon become apparent that big political issues loom. The general level of coverage will increase out of proportion to the normal trend.

If we assume that there will be a core of coverage, even though it may fluctuate at different times of the year, it is reasonable that effective press relations will take a greater share of the space normally made available for political comment at any one time.

If one political party uses the known level available to best advantage so much the better. Such activity may take a greater share or it may both take a greater share and create a larger volume of coverage (the size of the cake will increase). But knowing what is available and if the cake is growing will be important for both strategic and tactical planning.

Industrial applications for profile tracking

If all the cuttings from competing companies as well as the generic name of the product are included in analysis, the most likely level of coverage for this industry becomes apparent. A major increase in profile would be obvious and would indicate added effort on a noticeable scale by a competitor or, more likely, some kind of corporate upheaval in this industrial sector (Figure 8.6).

Armed with this information it is possible to look at share of available coverage and it is easy to spot the key players (Figure 8.6).

Tracking Press Coverage

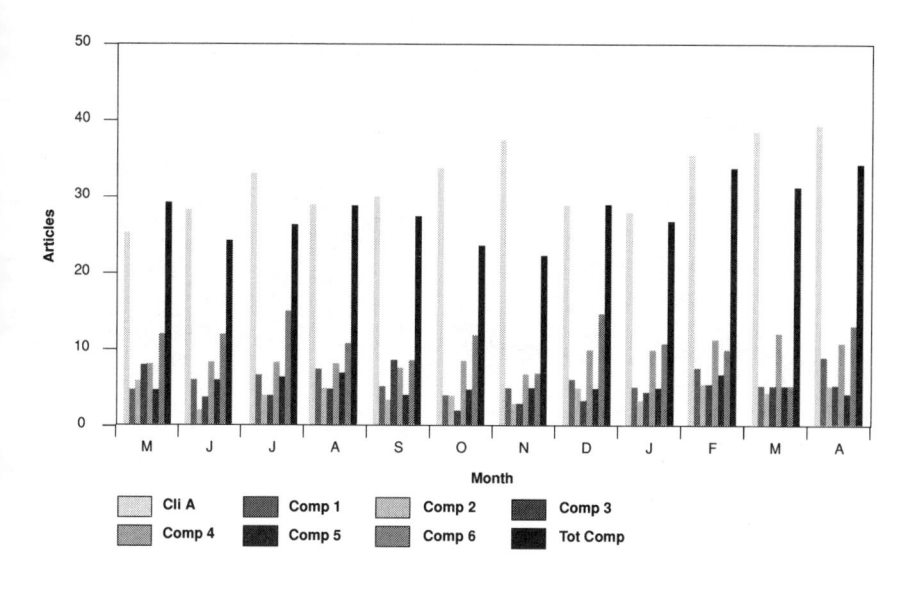

Figure 8.6 Client A: cuttings for client and competition

Not surprisingly the domestic British leader gets more coverage but more surprising is the low level of commitment to PR by its competitors. If they knew how badly they performed, what changes there may be with the leading company facing a planned press relations programme in short order.

Other measures underline how useful tracking is, if not critical.

Case study

A small sample was taken across three leading competitors to identify impact measures by simply giving a rating to each as follows:

name in headline	4
articles over 50 ccm	4
articles between 25–49 ccm	2
photograph	4
exclusive article	5

This provided a chart (Figure 8.7) which showed impact across all coverage and for each competitor. Here the fluctuations made analysis difficult without the average measure. The average measure is used to find out if there is a marked change or variance trend emerging. If so, there may be important news attached to the coverage or a new entrant to the market

Evaluating Press Coverage

place with better (or worse) writing styles. Investigation will quickly lead to identification of the reasons.

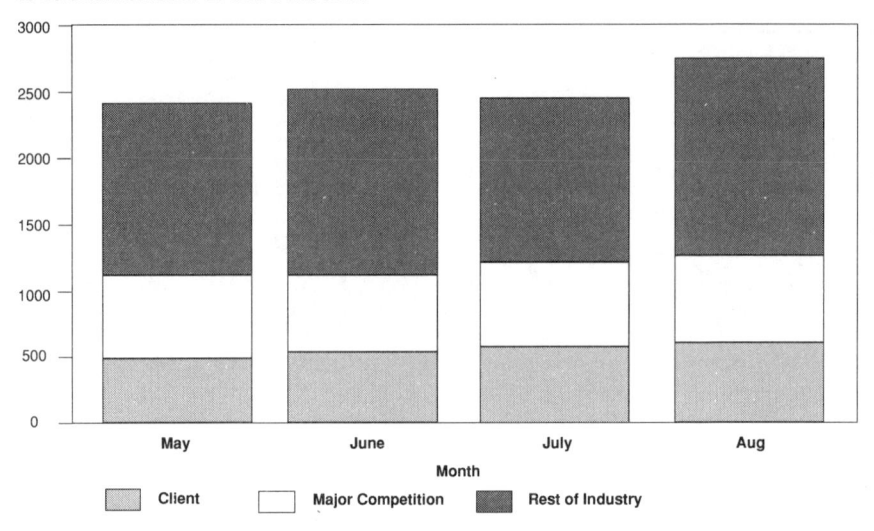

Figure 8.7 Total client industry coverage (ccm) over four months

While this chart is to hand you can put a weighted 'opportunities to enquire' measurement into the equation. The weighting is:

address or part of it in the copy?	3
telephone number provided?	4
reader enquiry number available?	5
response coupon?	5

The resultant graph shows that the heightened impact of one competitor in the middle of the chart was not attractive to the publications normally providing a reader enquiry service. In fact you are looking at the sale of the company.

This is confirmed by adding a measure of beneficial, neutral and adverse on the same chart. From this you can see that the writing was not only on the wall but in the journals long before the event. You can also see that by not increasing its presence after the acquisition, the company enabled its competitors to do better, with the market leader outdoing the rest. Here, failure to track the effect of coverage will be a threat for some time because the one company able to do most damage (the market leader) is in an even more powerful position.

For more day-to-day requirements each of the above examples can take you back to other measures.

Poor quality workmanship

Variance or trends in impact assessment will bring the public relations manager a view of the quality of the press campaign which may lead to a variety of conclusions. There may be a valid underlying problem which will need to be addressed such as the question of corporate image, historical problems with the media or poor performance from the press relations officer. However, before spending time and money finding out the reasons for changes in performance, there will be a reasonable foundation of fact on which to work.

Equally, if the actual enquiry level is not responding to the press campaign, a range of factors may be coming between the press image and performance. Sales enquiry response tracking can pose problems but can often lead the public relations consultant to decide if the press campaign is addressing the right problem. Constant recording of relevant information trends and variance will identify the existence of a problem long before it becomes critical.

Identifying issues

Even more can be gained when tracking follows a specific issue. Variance in reports will be one of the first indicators that the issue has become important but assessment of this importance is complicated. A huge adverse article can send a company running for cover but this may not always be necessary. The whole issue blows over.

The long, slow process of turning issues to advantage needs every available fact. Following the source and incidence of comment will quickly locate the requirement for immediate and long-term activity.

Tracking to aid resource allocation

As knowledge about the effects of press work improves with time so does the ability to make long-term judgements. In one case, a client was told by the consultancy that there was no point in trying to attract more coverage in the press. Maintenance at existing levels would be adequate. In addition the consultancy was able to point out that coverage would not diminish if less activity was maintained as long as major events were regularly programmed into the corporate and product press programmes. Budget resource could be allocated for greater effect in other areas of public relations. Much to the chagrin of the client, the consultancy could not offer the same level of measurement of effectiveness.

Press relations analysis for the marketeer

Public relations can make a major contribution to the body of research accessible to the marketeer. Experience worldwide is still not sufficient for total benefit to be gained from the data available but the means are there.

The budgets required for worthwhile impact can be large, and to optimise effect clients will need to make the investment in recording and tracking press relations performance. This may be an effort to achieve greater impact against budget available or to assess the effort required to gain a competitive edge. Without tracking, such conclusions have to be based on mere gut feeling.

Predicting coverage

So far, what has been discussed in this chapter is in fact the ability to predict press coverage. With historic precedent there is every reason to believe that this is possible and highly desirable for both client and consultancy. Many a consultant's reputation is based on an ability to achieve the right kind of coverage. The important issue now is the precision available.

Judgements must be made on:

- the stability of the organisations providing the interest for the journals;
- the likelihood of the product or issue being eclipsed by more significant coverage;
- reduction in the total published space available;
- increased interest in the subject matter;
- increased space available in the media;

Tracking Press Coverage

- more effort directed at the press by public relations consultants/organisations.

Most of these judgements will be based on advance information. If, for example, there is an upturn in advertising revenue, there will be increased editorial space available. If there is relevant news about the product or issue, it will gain added coverage.

Editorial space universe

If you start with a base line of coverage recorded for a year and call it 'editorial space universe' (ESU) you can flex this figure according to the known information which will change it. Tracking ESU will form the basis for much of the tracking required for the press programme planner (Figure 8.8).

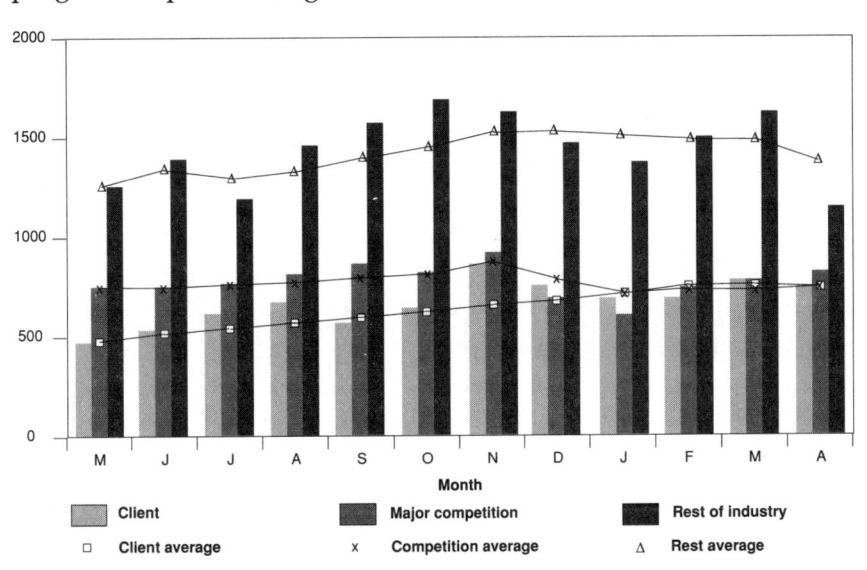

Figure 8.8 Total client industry coverage (ccm) over twelve months

The ESU will fluctuate from week to week and month to month. It will also have a cyclical nature, extra coverage coinciding with circumstances such as exhibitions, conferences, seasons of the year and political events. The odd peaks and troughs can be evened out; using rolling averages and straight line analysis the relevant data can be obtained. Equally it is possible to identify notable and predictable peaks and dips in ESU on a month by month basis.

Predicting peaks and troughs

Predictable variance can be a substantial trap for a press relations planner. A peak coinciding with an exhibition may increase the total of coverage available but it will also attract editorial matter from every professional and amateur publicist in sight. The total space available for a client will be squeezed by these other occasional entrants to the media. For this reason many public relations consultants avoid product launches at exhibitions. They simply cannot achieve the high relative coverage the new product deserves.

There are other factors to weigh when setting a base ESU.

The squeeze

If several organisations are working hard in the field and have good material for editors to use, then that subject will be given a higher proportion of coverage at the expense of another subject, issue or product. In other words the editorial space universe for this subject will grow.

If one of the press offices does not join in with added effort, it will see its coverage decline. It will be squeezed into a minor position. Once again the important measure of client plus competitor coverage comes to the rescue.

Spikes

We have all held press conferences on the day some other news was so important that our story sank without trace and we all benefit from the times when editors are desperate for any subject to write about to fill the publication. Many press offices exploit such times and achieve disproportionate coverage.

This kind of 'spike' in ESU is potentially always present and will need to be catered for in every press programme. Such spikes are also something of a problem in determining the true ESU.

For example, a major competitor event may generate substantial coverage which will thereby distort the figures quite dramatically. If the effort is sustained it has to be included in the overall figures. In many cases figures show an upsurge and then coverage declines as the competitor runs out of either budget or commitment.

Planning using ESU

In the end we achieve an ESU which can provide the basis for planning. It will show how much space *in the normal course of events* will be devoted to the subject in question (Figure 8.8). Planning press coverage around these opportunities in the ESU is not too difficult. We will by now have a reasonable idea of the number of articles, size, circulation achievable and impact available. Equally we will have a view of the space accessible in peripheral magazines.

Experience of the way in which press relations effort has an impact on ESU is now quite well understood. There is no doubt that an effective press campaign will take a bigger share of available coverage most of the time. Some consultancies are working on programmes where one objective is to apply sufficient pressure on the ESU that competitors effectively 'vanish' for prolonged periods.

The effect of this kind of squeeze is quite dramatic and we see coverage for competitors much reduced except at times of exhibitions and survey features when editors have to concentrate on spreading coverage among all contenders.

ESU in tertiary publications

It is tertiary coverage which is the most problematic. In a survey during 1989/90, one-third of published articles made the only reference to a certain product type in many publications in the year. Of that number (one third of the articles/journals), more than two-thirds did not cover the same product type in the second year.

The peripheral coverage for the subject included over 2500 ccm for the client. Almost none could be called wasted and, in the first year, one of the tertiary magazines proved to be the biggest enquiry puller of all time.

Such information is relevant to media planning as it is an important part of opinion forming and also a means of expanding the ESU. In the case quoted above almost all the peripheral coverage in the third year was about the client because the journals were targeted in the second and subsequent year with highly relevant press release material. Figure 8.9 is a pie chart showing proportion of coverage in one year against subsequent years.

Evaluating Press Coverage

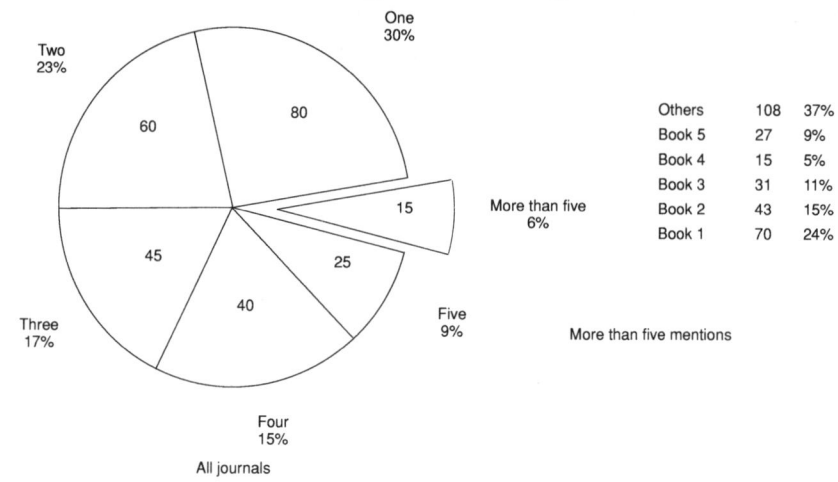

All journals

- One 30%
- Two 23%
- Three 17%
- Four 15%
- Five 9%
- More than five 6%

(Slice values: 80, 60, 45, 40, 25, 15)

More than five mentions

Others	108	37%
Book 5	27	9%
Book 4	15	5%
Book 3	31	11%
Book 2	43	15%
Book 1	70	24%

Figure 8.9 Journals covering client industry over two years

Predicting coverage as numbers of articles, words and ccm is effective to a degree. The precision will be quite accurate for the main line target publications but data becomes less accurate as the incidence of appearances diminishes in progressively more peripheral publications.

ESU providing other benefits

Once the less reliable media are filtered out during the monitoring process, other areas of measurement can be explored for likely opportunities.

Impact values will be very important to the marketeer. Here a much more even picture will emerge. There is little researched data available to date but several short-term surveys have been completed. It is interesting to note, for example, the frequency with which an address, or part of it, is identified and so on.

The ESU for selected spokespersons

There is no doubt that identifying the source for published material is both important and relevant. In many instances a campaign will be aimed at replacing a commonly used spokesperson with the client's own. Knowing which one to replace is easy if a long record of the common spokespeople is available. Predicting that a person will appear in print at some time in the year, or even regularly, allows us to select both the timing and subject matter to obtain maximum coverage.

Publishing formulae and coverage

Historic measures can be used to indicate future levels and types of coverage. The habits of the press die hard. The quality of prediction is as good as the success or otherwise of the formulae which make journals successful. Publications infrequently change the formulae which help us to predict, but when there is a change, it is identified through historical tracking and becomes part of future forecasting.

ESU for issues

To address another area which holds great potential it may be that such forecasting is not valid for products alone. There is every reason to believe that available ESU to cover issues can be tracked and by noting changing editorial attitudes and volume of coverage, the relevance of issues to the press is then available.

We all know this to be true. Major issues like world starvation, AIDS and drug abuse require significant effort to regain the headlines only weeks after they have been front page news. We do not have sufficiently long experience to identify the opportunities this offers to public relations practice but with publications wedded to successful publishing formulae the nature of editorial space universe committed to a particular readership does not change a great deal, except where interest is directed or a major issue like war takes a disproportionate level of coverage – even to the extent of increasing pages in newspapers. Using this knowledge, and known research methodology, some of the speculation about future media campaigns may soon become quite predictable.

City watch

Watching the proportion of ESU taken by different companies is interesting when compared with share values. There is no doubt that share prices progress as share of ESU grows and there is every reason to believe a predictive quality is evident in this type of monitoring.

Such systems are being used to good effect in the US. It is watching the relationship between coverage and share values which has led to a view that it takes four favourable units of press coverage to reverse one unit of adverse coverage.

A very interesting aspect is watching the coverage, size of article and circulation reach for a company change. With such image profile growth a company can be seen to be a very worthwhile investment.

13

Understanding Press Coverage for Effectiveness

Editorial impact

Throughout this book, there has been no real attempt to put a monetary value on press mentions. Part of the reason is that press coverage has a different effect on readers from that of other forms of promotion. Comparison nearly always shows the differences more than the similarities. The academic study of content analysis still has some way to go in establishing the difference between, say, advertising and editorial as it applies to the comparable effect on readers. Part of the problem is that much of the research is now quite old and the media, methodology and experience to hand has changed in the meantime. Where, at one time it was considered that content analysis could only provide information about content, experience is now showing that coverage can on its own, for example, change behaviour. To be able to show that a reader will not only be motivated to make an enquiry about a product because it appears in editorial, but that the motivation increases the numbers of people changing behaviour as a result of extra coverage is important. If extra share of coverage can show greater force behind behavioural change (and this is not fully proven), some new assumptions about what causes behavioural change can be made. Also by analysing coverage a change can be anticipated in the numbers of people motivated as share of coverage increases (Figures 4.5 and 4.6). As such evidence is confirmed from broader research and is refined, giving attributes to different types and volumes of editorial can be done more confidently.

Indeed, some academics believe that one of the disadvantages of content analysis is that it may not be representative of all editorial coverage of the subject in hand. This scepticism was based on some of the tracking in the USA which analysed a select number of high circulating newspapers. This is not necessarily true today now that with the use of computers the analysis is not confined to coverage in limited numbers of publications. Sampling today covers enormous numbers of publications.

With recent developments in measurement technology vast numbers of cuttings can be evaluated at very low cost to negate this argument. Equally there is an argument that coverage may not be representative because a publication may not use all the available material. This is not necessarily a problem if selection of the media is from a broad base and a greater opportunity is thereby created to explore a wider range of publications. Under such circumstances there is a better chance that printed material is more representative of the total story. The proposition in the story may then be available at a different level of detail to different audiences by virtue of the media each audience reads.

Measuring consumer trends?

The value of analysing content to give early clues to public opinion and actions has been tracked in the USA. It is hardly surprising to discover that the media foreshadows public response in a predictable way and that research confirms that media coverage can change the public's attitudes and behaviour in as little as two weeks or as much as six months.

John E Merriam, Chairman of the Conference on Issues and Media in Alexandria, Washington, showed that coverage of environmental news in the USA between 1984 and 1988 foreshadowed rising public demand for spending on environmental protection and dramatic growth in sales of organic foods. Interestingly, he found that specialist media offered the earliest clues and concluded 'If you want to know who's winning the computer wars, it makes sense to measure the exposure of different brands in popular computer magazines before you look in general circulation newspapers.'

The lag between consumers changing buying habits could be as much as six months. The USA experience suggests there is a direct relationship between coverage and consumer demand but, is a client prepared to maintain high expenditure to change attitudes and not be able to identify the effect for perhaps six months?

If one watches the circulation exposure of a particular subject, a company name for example, a rising star will show a progression over a period of time with some peaks which are slightly abnormal but with progressively less regression in both absolute numbers and reach of circulation compared to its competitors. During 1991 a Media Measurement customer was one such company. It is not a company quoted on the Stock Exchange and was not generating a profile for a quotation. For no apparent reason other than its growth, the company name doubled its circulation reach. Is this a result of some unarticulated public concern or interest?

Another company being tracked in a different industry but using identical methods also progressed its penetration of circulation and by a similar amount and equally for no apparent reason. Meantime two other companies, each one a competitor to the above, with very small circulation reach and low share of coverage by every measure when compared to their peers, were sold. Perhaps here the absence of media coverage, for whatever cause, had a predictive element.

Compare these stories with the sudden coverage in Germany at the time of the European Community Maastricht summit opposing monetary union for fear that the German currency would be threatened – which may well have been the media responding to an unarticulated public concern.

Is it true then, that the media foreshadows public response, or responds to unarticulated public concern? There is an element of truth in both and as stories come to prominence the nature of the proposition frequently changes en route. But it is not just an increase in coverage which is indicative of important events.

It is not only that if the public has a worry that when the media articulates this concern it strikes a chord and becomes a major issue. There are many other factors at work. A frequent reason for added share of coverage (which probably has greater effect on behaviour than sheer exposure) is that a previous competitor for coverage has gone very quiet for some reason.

Perhaps if the cold war was still a major issue some other aspect of media concern would not be apparent. Is this to suppose that public concern over an issue so excluded would not be awaiting mass coverage and therefore wide public debate? Experience suggests not and as more evidence comes to hand from measuring the breadth and diversity of the press, we shall see more evidence of the presence of coverage as well as its absence as being indicative of impending change.

Expressing complex ideas to a wide audience

Beyond the disputed fact that editorial coverage is, frequently, less expensive than advertising, there is evidence that focused coverage is far more believable and acceptable to readers than an advertisement. Certainly, as long as the subject matter is interesting and newsworthy, editorial is more pervasive for the same budget. Press relations work often reaches more journals (and hence a wider readership) than any other form of promotion.

In addition it is frequently more detailed and can convey a proposition with greater clarity. Its great attribute is an ability to explain the complexity of many products and propositions and in that respect it also carries third party endorsement, by association, with the publication and is seen to be more credible and hence more persuasive.

Press coverage is in many ways more subtle. The key benefits and product USPs can be stated in a more indirect way, using actual examples to demonstrate a point, than the 'high impact' approach normally used in advertising.

To produce a range of advertisements that covers the requirements of all products and propositions plus corporate issues over a suitable spread of journals is not only difficult to achieve but extremely expensive. This is not the case with press material. Measuring comparable appearances with more focused publicity mechanisms obviously has value.

A perceived virtue

Editorial space is also keenly contested by a company's rivals. For a company to be seen to be active in the market-place by all potential purchasers, even those that have little current purchasing intention, it is necessary to fight for that space with as much vigour and determination as for new orders. It must always be remembered that beneficial press coverage has great virtue in the reader's eye.

With such differences in purpose, much press relations work cannot be compared to other kinds of promotion. The selection of media needs to be different and the mechanism to measure effectiveness has to be very distinct. While there is an excellent argument for measuring press coverage against such norms as opportunities to read, product enquiries and sales, such analysis is too narrow to be effective. Indeed, there is significant evidence to show that press campaigns designed to achieve such narrow objectives are not particularly cost effective.

So how does one establish the effectiveness of press relations work? The obvious measures of pre- and post- campaign opinion polling and akin research can go only part of the way, particularly as they are frequently confused by other promotional 'noise'. In addition all too often the client requires a measure similar to the mores of advertising and in particular wants to see a result on the bottom line.

Measure enquiries

Press coverage has significant residual impact on subsequent publicity exposure and both are heavily conditioned by other experiences such as word of mouth, exposure to the product and subsequent competitive coverage.

Case study

The efficacy of press mentions provided over 20 per cent of all new sales leads for a capital plant manufacturer and achieved more than 10 per cent market share from a zero start. After the first year, presence at exhibitions and advertising provided too much promotional noise for this case to be followed without considerable difficulty but the combination led to 25 per cent market penetration over a three year period and sales in excess of £10 million.

The tracked coverage (mentions, ccm, photographs, opportunities to read) was always more than three times that of the leading competition.

The effectiveness of this press campaign is measurable for the enquiries it generated but whether this would have been achieved with a smaller share of ESU and how many sales enquiries were generated by salespersons' efforts supported by result of press coverage is uncertain. Measuring effectiveness could have been achieved by measuring sales enquiries. Alternatively the real measure for effectiveness, and probably the most accurate, is share of ESU.

While there is research which allows comparisons to be drawn between advertising and different press relations campaigns, the nature of each case will make a qualitative answer difficult to find.

An effective medium

Research into the effect violence on television has on the audience shows that media coverage cannot be assessed in isolation and equally the effectiveness of media coverage for communicating with different audiences is subject to the audience type in mind.

To begin with, the potential of the media as a communications channel has to be considered. As a generalisation, the better educated an audience, the greater the likelihood of the written media being an effective message carrier. In addition, the greater exposure in multiple media, the greater the effect.

Thus, reaching an educated and articulate audience through serious national newspapers, highbrow publications and specialist journals may be very effective. In public relations terms, there is a strong case for exploring other media for communication. For our educated audience this will not necessarily include television and, if it does, programme selection will be important as such an audience will not be as dedicated to this medium as a less well-educated audience. This does not imply that television is the only mass communication medium for less well educated audiences.

What is, therefore, important is to assess coverage against the medium most likely to have, or to have had, the greatest effect on the audience. Such an effect, however, is not based solely on the amount of coverage but whether the coverage has been targeted to influence that mass audience.

The specialist press

There is a tendency for much evaluation to be concentrated on national media but it is not the best way of evaluating coverage. There are two reasons: First, the ESU is narrow and second the coverage will most often be drawn from old news rewritten.

Watching a wide range of journals, tracking the number of stories and circulation (reach) about an industry or issue gives an excellent view of the progress of such stories, identifies opportunities to progress them and reduces the time taken to spot trends. Faster identification and a wider view overcomes many of the perceived difficulties in measuring effect.

The specialist, trade and local press is an important area for monitoring and has a predictive quality.

Addressing a knowledge gap

There is also a consideration of the motivation for readership. A press relations campaign which exposes a gap in audience knowledge will motivate that audience to find out more. The expression 'new' in much press coverage seems to have this effect and tends to generate sales leads. If knowledge is at a low level, the treatment of the subject by the media will have a greater impact on the reader. Thus, in measuring coverage it is important to find media which identify the information gap and then to track coverage to find out how it is presenting information or 'the solution' to the audience. A campaign which sets out to identify a knowledge gap and then provides the media with the ammunition to answer the questions will score very highly. If, however, the message is unpleasant or uncomfortable to the audience, it will tend to look for and 'select' information which is not so uncomfortable and which supports beliefs, attitudes and values extant.

In evaluating coverage, there is substantial evidence to suppose that the following considerations are valid:

- definition of audiences as: highly targeted, opinion forming and penumbral;
- definition of knowledge gap;
- multimedia evaluation;
- efficacy measure in exposure of knowledge gap;
- quality and quantity of media reach in exposing knowledge gap;
- quantity of media reach in providing information to fill knowledge gap;
- quality of coverage in terms of comfort in filling knowledge gap.

To turn this into a measurement which is commercially useful will depend on objectives set at the beginning of a campaign.

An example of how a campaign run along such lines would work might be for the introduction of a material which has specific waterproof and breathing qualities. The objective is to promote the product into wider markets.

In the imaginary case of a cloth manufacturer: research will first examine an audience we shall call specifiers, approvers and decision makers. A six month evaluation of all coverage on the subject of waterproof clothing with subclassifications enquiring after breathing qualities, waterproof treatments and outdoor wear will reveal what competitors, manufacturers and fashion correspondents have written on the subject. In addition key journals and journalists will emerge with a list of industry commentators.

With this information it is possible to identify what the market needs to know about this and similar products (eg easy manufacture, colour fastness, comfort etc).

The campaign will cover the total audience in phase one, which explains market need and benefits of materials with the specification of the new product. This will be measured to find out when the story has been accepted in the key journals. At that time the product launch and subsequent analysis will look for coverage which describes the product meeting the market need. This will be followed by case study press work which explains the benefits of use by manufacturers, designers and fashion houses.

The knowledge gap and information to fill it are carefully monitored throughout and a wary eye is kept on competition. In such a case different parts of the media will be used to impart selected components in the story at timed intervals. Without prior media coverage research, the effectiveness of the campaign will not be as thorough. Indeed, there will be no way of knowing the size of the ESU and as a result how much coverage should be expected in order to rise above all the other relevant coverage in the same field.

Case study

In the case of an industrial equipment supplier, there is a simple example of how press relations works when the criteria are based on meeting public relations, as opposed to advertising, objectives.

The audience was technically oriented and worked in a specific field. At a time when maintaining stock in its industry was considered a liability and fast throughput important, it was the consultant's job to identify the client's alternative to commonly used systems and competitors' products which were being sold as high-tech goods. The client's product was more advanced than its competition.

The normal means of communication, trade journals and academia, were used for the first part of the campaign to expose the knowledge gap.

It prompted the media to explain the shortcomings of past practice but, because the obvious target publications were either wedded to existing systems or were putting forward uncomfortable alternatives (uncomfortably high tech, complex and expensive), it was used as a secondary medium for explaining the alternative and new products.

A further group of publications, more closely associated with automated systems and quality management, was sought, which covered the same audience but (mostly) in different subject areas (using magazines with more horizontal coverage) and the proposition of an effective alternative which, although substantially automated (and more so than its competitors), was presented in the press as being up to date and neither too complex nor too expensive.

Thus, the vertical trade press outlined the problem and offered a high-tech solution which compounded the frustration of the prospective customer. Several other magazines published simple stories about solutions to the problem.

Measuring press effectiveness in selected publications was based on all coverage across a wide range and was monitored against enquiries to type of journal. This ensured that the appropriate message was understood by the audience. The principal publication in the field almost totally ignored the campaign and kept plugging away at the problem to seek a solution. It was two years before it recognised how effective the coverage had been and what it had missed.

In the meantime, competitors were frequently promoting standard (and old fashioned) solutions with complex attachments or electronics and their alternative automation expertise. Both messages were alienating their target audience. As they lost market share they compounded the mistake with additional 'high tech' press and advertising coverage.

As enquiries and sales were generated for the client, case study material was used through all available media with comforting statements which centred on simple product features and operational benefits. Market leadership ensued.

The value of press mentions in such a case is in the ability to progress a message but it was understanding the audience need that was critical.

In such cases there are few up-front financial measures but the messages had to be on target in order to differentiate the product from similar, if less modern or complex, competitor products. The campaign was aimed at journals covering the most technically advanced products but the stories were written not to show off these features but the benefits and in a style which did not concentrate on on-board computers. Some skill was needed to get the coverage, in view of the low-tech content in press releases about the products, and fortunately the competitors were trying to sell technology in the wrong (trade) publications.

Finding and exploiting the gap

Since press relations has greater reach per pound and can explain complex issues in different ways to different audiences, knowledge gap promotion is one of its most effective applications.

For such forceful promotion to be effective, careful monitoring is more important than ever. The techniques required are the same as for issue tracking. Here too we look at competing issues which include the traditional and fashionable icons of the day. In addition we ask the question 'why not buy' in market research and track corresponding coverage. When the 'why not buy' does not make sense we have identified the knowledge gap. It is prudent to research further before embarking on the press campaign.

With all knowledge gap press relations work, identifying publications reaching appropriate audiences is vital. Some publications will be well outside the normal press list used historically and considerable creativity is required to ensure effective coverage.

For this type of campaigning tracking coverage is critical. The sequence of events has to be orderly as the audience will not comprehend the knowledge gap until it is explained and will, therefore, not be anxious to fill it. The impact of the coverage designed to fill a gap in information will fall flat on its face if the reader is unaware of a knowledge deficiency.

14
International Press Programmes

Public relations' practice follows common rules in Europe and the USA and, even in countries where language and cultural differences might be thought to present problems, many press measures remain constant and effective. The opportunity to translate evaluation techniques across language and cultural frontiers is a fascinating prospect; attention to similarities rather than differences helps here.

In most countries the formats of newspapers and specialist publications follow conventional patterns and methods for capturing attention are much the same. The front page is a common measure, as is the presence of editorial, which is normally distinguishable from advertising copy. A photograph or headlined name has impact across the world, while the relative size of an article has the same meaning in Russia as in France.

It would, however, not be sensible to compare coverage between cultures. While one culture might be adept at creating and using 'sound bites' backed up with expert editorial analysis, the same impact will be created in another culture by printing the full text of a long speech.

With such provisos in mind, several common systems for comparing effect of editorial coverage and press relations work are possible.

Performance-related press relations

Since measurement can be expressed as comparable between countries, the concept of performance-related press relations is eminently translatable.

Imagine such a proposal coming before a company beginning to spread its activities into a new territory. In such circumstances, the press office can present a proposal to ensure a press presence to assist with the marketing effort with the prospect of achieving results hitherto beyond belief. By setting relatively low targets, the press relations manager will not be involved in detailed research but can specify what is newsworthy, needs coverage, why, when and where and then, how much.

Across many cultures, material generated by a home campaign will form a core of information for an overseas press agent. With a small element of new on-territory generated press material, a fixed-cost campaign can be measured against actual press coverage achieved. The financing of international press relations can be reduced to the cost of a press office. It will not incur the higher overheads of an on-territory public relations consultant and local expertise in measuring results will grow very quickly.

As a proposition the idea of setting overseas press coverage attainment targets is new. For years we have all been issuing press releases to overseas subsidiaries and dealers, often to little effect. There is no guessing how much good press material dies in the hands of on-territory managers who frequently have many roles, often in the sales area. Equally, there is little incentive to translate and transcribe and the job never gets done.

Case study

An American multinational was in the habit of issuing case studies and product material across the world. The UK publicity manager found this material difficult to understand and hired a local public relations consultancy, believing it would prepare more suitable material for British use. The consultancy, on finding this mine of useful information, used 80 per cent of the US output. When transcribed, interpreted and anglicised it made a major contribution to a successful UK press campaign.

Of course, it is unrealistic to expect too much from press attainment targets. One of the main problems is locating a trustworthy organisation capable of measuring press coverage to reasonably common standards. The incidence of reliable press cutting bureaux is high in most countries although not always as comprehensive as it might be. Sourcing cuttings is not too difficult; the real problem is finding common measures.

Common measures

Common features of coverage include:

- number of cuttings;
- ccm;
- impact – headline, photograph etc;
- attribution;
- source;
- exclusivity;
- multiple source/multiple byline;
- BNA.

These features can be used to assess the quantity and quality of coverage and can measure effectiveness of overseas press relations activity. This principle is effective and a number of contracts have been let to press agents using such measures.

Database deficiency

The incidence of usable database information to provide the data required to support software varies from country to country and there is not yet a comprehensive international source available. In the UK, the ability to match substantial amounts of information about publications providing press mentions is very useful but is dependent on electronically held information to keep cost low.

The absence of electronic data in other countries need not be too detrimental but can mean that the totality of measurement will not be universal for all territories. Indeed, some of the coverage will need to be analysed by hand.

Difference in style

Sensitivity to the differing editorial styles of the media in other countries has to be borne in mind.

The very newsy style of the French, the quantified and technical detail of the Germans and the occasionally brutal expressions of the Italians are examples of pitfalls to be avoided. In addition the relationship between advertising and editorial copy is not as easily distinguished in many countries as it is in the UK. The disingenuous habit of newspapers and magazines to cloak advertising in editorial style is to be deplored in every instance but is becoming part of the advertising mix in many countries, even to the eternal shame and detriment of the British popular newspapers. It is not uncommon to find so-called editorial written by staff journalists which is a straight puff for a product. This attempt to fool readers has its counterpart among PR practitioners submitting programme or product information which should be included in advertising copy but is passed off as news or for editorial inclusion.

Without using a database of journals (which is, however, available) a case study of what can be achieved in independent editorial coverage is illustrated below:

Case study

The analysis of French press cuttings procured from a UK bureau astonished the French managing director when he was invited to a seminar on group public relations in an international company.

He found that from the UK it had been possible both to quantify competitor prevalence in the French press and the virtual non-existence of his own company's coverage. He was even more surprised to be given the names of three prospective consultancies who were prepared to use British generated material to win 10 per cent of the French media coverage in the industry-related publications. The fixed price cost was 10 per cent of the advertising spend on territory.

The manager who organised this arrangement, and who did not speak a word of French, set the coverage target as the number of mentions and ccm.

The arrangement is working well and on target, with market share showing notable signs of improvement.

This illustration of what can be achieved may be basic but it has been very effective. Its great advantage is that the cost of sourcing information for use in press releases is much reduced as it is applied across multiple territories.

There is one known example of a German company contracted to a British press relations agency on a performance-related fee contract.

International contract considerations

In specifying press relations campaigns overseas there are financial and contractual considerations which need attention.

In the first instance, international law is not very helpful when dealing with the flow of copyright. The aim is to present material to an overseas agent with the express intention for it to be translated and transcribed for use on-territory. It is important that the copyright remains in the hands of the principal at every stage.

In addition, when a foreign language is involved, there is no substitute for a resident specialist who can check, verify and approve copy. A copy of the final press release will need to be issued both to the local resident and the international manager in charge of the press relations campaign.

This is not a simple translation exercise. Translated press releases are hardly ever acceptable to the local media and are open to wide misinterpretation.

Identifying a suitable partner overseas is not always simple but the advent of *Hollis Europe* has made the task much easier than hitherto. Using this reference publication it is possible to identify consultancies with experience in the relevant field.

There is no case for attempting to introduce a performance-related campaign to any consultancy without first showing how coverage is to be measured and the methods to be used. Equally the negotiations have to be face to face and on-territory.

Full references need to be taken up and client references will need to be carefully followed through.

An alternative is to use one of the international groupings of consultancies but the same rules apply and can be somewhat tortuous. The one great benefit is that it is usually easy to talk to a number of consultants at the same time during one of their regular meetings.

Conducting trials

Having been through this hoop of finding the appropriate partner, it is important to conduct closely monitored trials. Before a campaign is involved it is essential that differences in interpreting the results are ironed out. Examples of pitfalls include even simple things such as the method used for measuring attributable mentions (keyword occurrences or articles containing keywords etc).

While there are European evaluation services available and new ones being developed to monitor media effectiveness, there is no well-recognised service reaching into every country. This means that the press office wishing to develop such concepts either has to find a suitable existing operation or will need to develop a system from scratch.

Developing a system

An example of the kind of contract required is given in Appendix 2 and may be helpful but will need to be put to a qualified legal expert for individual territories and, of course, for much of Europe it will need to be Notarised.

For the time being the assessment of press campaign effectiveness across Europe is dependent on a few consultancies and even fewer in-house departments with evaluation systems covering particular subjects and issues.

To be able to run press campaigns planned from analysing historic data to the levels currently available in the UK is neither common nor yet practical without more experience. However, with the evaluation tools currently to hand, an effective start has been made and considerable expertise will be available in the very near future.

15
Politics and Coverage

The area of effectiveness monitoring in a political context provides several examples which can be translated into many other applications for effective monitoring.

To monitor all the press for all the coverage about politics is a gargantuan task and will not be a common or permanent activity among political institutions. With political comment about numerous political parties represented on (and/or campaigning to be elected to) assemblies as diverse as the European Parliament and a parish council, the logistics for comprehensive evaluation are, to all intents and purposes, too great.

As one might expect, there has been substantial post-election analysis of coverage looking for bias and as academic research. There is not a great deal of published evidence of coverage being statistically evaluated during an election campaign or being used as a management tool in the conduct of political press campaigns during an election. To date, most political parties depend on their 'intelligence' systems to feed and filter relevant political news; not the most scientific analysis but better than none.

The overnight analysis of coverage run by the major political parties still favours a view of key journalists and publications and so the statistics are taken from a very narrow base. Many commentators believe that the press, more than anything, expresses unarticulated public concern and this is probably true of national media. After all, the editorial in national newspapers is researched and written by a small number of journalists many of whom are dependent on what they themselves read and a handful of contacts. Compared with the hundreds, if not thousands, of journalists in the regional and specialist press influenced by an even wider and more diverse number of contacts, the wider press is more interesting. The opportunity for the analyst to see an issue emerging or pressure group at work at grass-roots level through wide analysis is greater. In time such issues will gain greater visibility and may well become important to the national media.

Measuring coverage, and especially circulation reach, about companies and new products suggests that the nationals take some time to pick up a story which is already popular elsewhere.

Selective political analysis

Total media evaluation during a campaign is still too great a task but what is valuable is selective analysis to encompass views on political leaders and party spokespersons, particular elections, significant issues and sensitive constituencies and regions.

Popularity of policies and issues

The amount of media coverage is sufficiently large to track, very accurately, the popularity of politics, politicians, policies and issues in the media. There is not yet sufficient data to see how the ebb and flow of coverage moves through the seasons and what the total 'editorial space universe' (ESU) is at any one time.

This is going to be a very interesting area for future analysis and for measuring party political share of available media space, the share awarded to different politicians and different issues. Identification of relative coverage gained by parties and, in particular, individual politicians will be very revealing. Work in the USA has been conducted for more than a decade as an academic exercise and more information is beginning to come to light.

Identifying the politically famous

From such an analysis it will become increasingly easy to find the best political self-publicists and to judge who will have important future political careers. Equally, among the thrusting publicists, statistical analysis will show where established leaders can look for the greatest threat.

The presence of a high national and regional profile for politicians will also become evident and 'source' analysis will show up many back room political influencers.

Tracking pressure groups

Among the uses for this type of analysis will be tracking the effectiveness of new political parties and pressure groups. The media acceptance of their standpoint and the effect on established political institutions can now be followed with relative ease.

Tracking issues

For the campaign manager, tracking issues will be a boon. It will quickly become apparent who is winning the arguments and who is shaping opinion most. Comparing differing issues as covered in the press will show where policy is under attack and from whom. It will show which issues are catching the imagination of the media and, often, who is responsible.

Comparisons of individual politicians will also provide the information to identify who best to use to front an issue or policy change and how effective they are in the press.

Regional analysis will identify variance with national trends on particular policies and the relative strengths of politicians and parties in addressing these differences.

Effectiveness of messages and regional targeting

The effectiveness of statements aimed and targeted at the regions can now be measured in terms of the number of households which had an opportunity to read, the impact of the article on the page and the frequency of exposure. And knowing the message is getting across will be immensely useful for tactical deployment of key spokespersons.

Identify regional strengths or weakness

By looking at regional and local press, strengths and weaknesses in political organisations will become apparent and party managers will be able to beef up weak areas ahead of elections to turn electoral opportunities to advantage.

Ability to react overnight

The speed with which national newspapers can be analysed will mean that the popularity of different issues and commentary about campaign management can be assessed overnight and responses on morning radio and television can be prepared and acted upon. The politician, at the morning briefing, will be able to lead press opinion from a position of great strength, knowing not only the headline issues, but where underlying media views are changing.

Identify the unexpected journalists

During election campaigns, specialist political commentators are supplemented by hundreds of journalists drafted in to cover stories. Here is a band of reporters relatively unknown to political managers. Spotting the ones with new views and media influence will be quick and effective using press coverage analysis.

For those preparing commentaries for consumption overseas, a whole new method of assessment is wide open. Politicians coming to the fore, important issues and the relative strengths of parties nationally and regionally can quickly be identified and commented upon.

Press assessment – a news story in its own right

Press assessment itself will be a campaign issue. Who is winning and who is losing will be watched and presented with great glee when weaknesses show that leaders are not effective in making the running. And the press will be in there too. Picking winners and losers will be easier and some politicians will be surprised at the size and enthusiasm of the press corps around them. Others will be horrified.

Those lovely programmes where the media watches the media will have a whole new dimension. The old system of reviewing what the papers said will be enhanced and accusations of bias and overkill will add to the daily excitement. Long hours of waiting for the results to come in will include a blow-by-blow account of how people and issues explode and die as the campaign progresses.

In the aftermath, analysis by both winners and losers will include a much more accurate assessment of how political parties handled the press. Over time, and it could be some way off, all this will be achieved using a combination of different press monitoring surveys over different timescales. To date, the knowledge base for this type of activity is tiny and more experience will be available as the practice grows.

Country coverage

Effectiveness monitoring can also take place in a national context. For example, how good is the US Embassy at winning over the British press and the hearts and minds of British opinion formers? One doubts if even the US Embassy really knows. It could – and quite easily. So too could all nations with a presence in the UK. Indeed, measuring not only the coverage about countries, but their culture, economic activity and a whole host of other issues is very simple.

What applies to an embassy also applies to the British Foreign Office. What are attitudes in the British press to the Argentine or to trade sanctions on Iraq and what is their media's view of Britain? For students of press relations evaluation these rhetorical questions are an illustration of the broad-based use and value of monitoring the media and identify some of the information available and the effective use to which it can be put.

All manner of issue management and coverage analysis is available to an embassy. While there are readers in most embassies looking for information which is of use and interest to nations overseas, a mechanism to evaluate this information and to maintain a view of how the media regards a country is either a question of feel or opinion research. Media monitoring with evaluation is a valuable intermediate step.

It is particularly valuable when monitoring specific attitudes. There is every reason, for example, to monitor the media for its coverage and attitudes to trade, technology, culture, arts and so forth. In this kind of research an embassy will not only identify differing views but the people who influence what is written.

One speculates about the use to which an embassy might put press coverage evaluation. One such field may be in the comparative presence of coverage about important industries. For example, many countries compete for British tourists. It is important for the embassy to ensure that organisations which assist in promoting tourism take an important part of the ESU. Knowing how effective tour operators are in the press and how they deal with issues affecting the tourist trade will be valuable to add to the general coverage in a targeted manner, assist the tour operators with relevant briefing for added coverage and to identify those journalists and sources who can most influence the media.

Alternatively though, analysis in countries such as the USA can be used by the British Embassy to identify coverage about British industries. Additionally, some trade associations may want to find out similar data. One envisages a circumstance when such trade associations may well pursue the Foreign Office with such facts and invite added government help in putting their case in, to maintain the example, the USA.

Attitudes to national policies

The regard for countries' leaders, policies and products is all important and, where countries and nations are in the limelight, this is very valuable.

The changing media attitudes to the former Soviet Union are fascinating and for countries like Poland can be important as it continues to look for friends outside the old Soviet sphere of influence. It is not just the attitudes of the major newspapers which are important. Many other publications such as magazines, local newspapers and ethnic journals help provide a clear overall picture.

It is through such monitoring that attitudes can be evaluated and an assessment of the pressures on government and institutions made. The ability to identify writers and sources for the writers provides a clear view of the people who most shape the ideas we have about foreign countries.

16

Corporate Coverage and Issue Management

The impact of the media on major corporations requires skilled handling. Those organisations which, even five years ago, eschewed a corporate affairs department have now come to realise that there is a requirement for close observation and direction of the diversity and pervasiveness of the media.

'Watch dog' organisations, inside and outside government, are increasingly using the media to affect business and frequently use the press as the first line of contact.

Electronic databases are making research on large organisations quick and cheap and, with very open annual reports, the impact of events on a small subsidiary can quickly have a significant effect on the corporate business environment.

The corporate citizen

There is also a growing trend which views major companies as corporate citizens. Here there is a requirement for evaluation which affects and influences internal activities. Until recently, it was impossible to assimilate every relevant article published in the media. Understanding what total effect the media had on a corporation was logistically hopeless. This is now changing and, in the 1990s, media coverage evaluation is valuable for tracking performance of the corporation and its competitors.

News affects investors

Media monitoring covering investment news has become more important with the increasing numbers of both private and institutional investors. Inward investment from overseas and the private investor is influenced to a great degree by the media requiring added investor relations activity beyond London-based institutions.

Using electronically held news libraries, which are available to everyone, plus the financial institutions' own investment data, now held on computers, it is possible to gather immense amounts of information about companies in a few minutes. At the same time it is easy to find out how well reported and how well regarded a corporation and its subsidiary organisations may be throughout the trade and technical media.

Whereas in the past the corporate affairs office will have read newspapers and cuttings to gain an overall view, the sheer weight of press comment now makes this task time consuming and onerous.

A simple monitor, showing how much coverage and identifying variance to the norm for coverage over a wide spectrum of journals, both reduces the time taken in reading and provides a very valuable insight into how the organisation is regarded and its effectiveness in putting a case to investors compared to other companies.

Predicting share values

The movement of share of editorial space universe between competitors is a mechanism with a variety of uses. By looking at the performance of products and services between a quoted company and its direct competitors an excellent view of its performance is available. Thus a quoted British company can be compared in its British market-place to other local and international competitors. So far the volume of data is not sufficient to be certain, but there appears to be a predictive quality about press coverage which is interesting and is largely confirmed by research published in the USA.

While the initial cost of setting up analysis for industrial sectors will be quite high, the market for such a service is substantial. There is already an experimental system which looks at competing subsidiaries and assesses the pervasiveness of these companies in their fields. Over six months a pattern emerges between winners and losers. Thereafter, any fluctuation can be indicative of the changing nature of a company. By rating individual subsidiaries in its industry, the value of the company as a whole (and its brands) in the eyes of the media (frequently 90 or more expert press commentators) becomes evident.

In the past, monitoring all the media, and particularly the specialist media, has been too expensive to make such comparisons possible and so national newspapers have usually been the yardstick. There is very strong evidence that the specialist media pre-empts the national news media by as much as six months. Complementing existing services, a significantly greater predictive analysis will shortly be available to investors.

Monitor brand image

Monitoring can also be used to value the media conception of brands and subsidiaries both as part of the group image and compared to other brands. At the same time it is useful for measuring the effectiveness of brand management and company promotion as part of managing total corporate image.

With goodwill for brand names now a balance sheet asset, proving its maintenance is all important. Press coverage evaluation is not a true measure without a comparable bench-mark and so comparative or competitor measures are significant, as is a measure of beneficial, neutral and adverse. Indeed, with few effective measures for brand image value assessment this can be a significant method for valuation.

The need to monitor brand image is important in its own right and there is every reason to believe that the press will provide a constant view of how the image is perceived among opinion formers. This is a measure which is ahead of the market and provides a good view of how brand marketing is proceeding. It is also a valuable means of watching competing brands and will identify effectiveness. Here is an early warning system which can help corporate management.

Corporate image contribution

The contribution a Group makes to its subsidiaries and the return provided from divisions is not only measured in financial support and contribution. The effectiveness of management style and the contribution of a subsidiary to Group image are also important considerations. The tales of subsidiaries straying from the fold are legion and are reflected in the way a subsidiary presents itself to the press. With consistent monitoring, a corporation is able to identify the level of effort a subsidiary is putting behind press relations and the contribution such effort is making to the Group as a whole. Corporate identity monitoring requires constant vigilance and while the logo and style can be closely followed, the contribution through media such as the press is more difficult to gauge.

Managing subsidiary PR effectiveness

In the past, few corporate affairs managers have been in a position to assess how much and how effective their subsidiary companies' press relations activity really is. Now it is possible to view subsidiary company coverage not just as a handful of press cuttings but against competitors and between press officers. When one looks across the press relations expenditure of some of the larger company groupings, the total can reach astronomic proportions. There are many British companies with total press relations expenditure in excess of £1 million which goes unreported and unmeasured. Collecting and collating the data on expenditure is not nearly so hard when monitoring is achieved through effectiveness measurement rather than the more common monitor of the number of press releases issued or consultancy fees paid!

With this information easily monitored, a measure of the level of awareness and impact can be ascertained. Managing public relations results in this context can also include cost effectiveness.

Issue management

One of the key uses for monitoring is in the field of issue management. Many companies need to be aware of issues and how they are dealt with in the media. To know what is being said and by whom and from what angle is invaluable. To be able to track such coverage is a boon. For a large part of the time the agenda is set by others and the story has its own momentum.

The cost of such tracking is minuscule compared to the value of the data available. It is particularly useful when competitor watching.

Research is the first area for effective action and a really good problem will mean a lot of press coverage needs to be read and processed before any effective programme can begin.

Research

Sometimes the requirement is very urgent and reading up on the subject needs two distinct approaches. The first is to look to the media and the second to the best published authorities.

The quick and easy way to find out the media and sources to choose is to analyse past coverage. Using computer based analytical systems covers a lot of ground. Alternatively, in-house assessment can achieve the same, or more closely focused, analysis.

Comparing issues

The enormity of an issue will be seen from the coverage given. At an early stage it is worth selecting similar issues to compare the editorial space universe taken up by each. One can then monitor how the issue waxes and wanes in the media and bring a sense of proportion to all considerations in the matter. Every issue has a core concept and is approached through different topics. If one angle is not providing good copy, journalists will try another. Watching such approaches is important.

Find out reach

The next priority is to ascertain the reach of the subject throughout the media. Coverage in the national dailies will be reflected in some other publications and this reach will be important in planning a response. It will frequently also identify particular and relevant journalists and campaigners.

If the issue is very live there will be photographic coverage and how much will indicate attitudes in different media. But it is in the lists of journalists and the references to sources where the most important data will be found. It is these lists which will provide the starting point for action in and outside the media.

Identify sources

It is important to identify attitudes and the quality of the grasp these public voices have of issues through assessment of the coverage.

Within 24 hours it is possible to have a good view of the principal players affecting national newspaper coverage and to identify which articles must be read first. In addition, tracking the sources will provide a starting point for where to look for more serious tracts and publications on the matter. Few publications will fail to credit published source material. In a few hours all this information analysis will have saved much time and effort and is very valuable if an issue is suddenly forced upon a client.

While it will be of paramount importance to maintain a close watch on all coverage it will also be important not to miss trends in the coverage.

Tracking share of voice

The importance of the issue will be reflected in press coverage and tracking total coverage, reach of circulation and share of editorial space universe will give an excellent feel for the popularity of the subject. Watching changes of stance in individual and all publications will also be invaluable. Identifying the force behind an argument is not easy when there is an emotional attachment; analysis will help cool heads.

Monitor others

At the same time there will be a number of other players in the field. Their output and the nature of coverage they attract can be monitored in both actual coverage read and as part of monitoring trends and new topics as they are brought to bear on the issue.

We have already seen the kind of coverage monitoring available but it is in the area of new angles where tracking can be most useful.

Constant measuring

A strategic response will need to be decided and monitoring will, of course, be part of the package. Selecting the criteria will be important and it is seldom worthwhile abandoning one line of research in favour of another. It is better to maintain the early analysis criteria and to add more. In this way tracking is effective because greater experience is available and comparative measures are maintained.

Issues have a long life and to be in the centre can be an exhausting business. If an issue is also adverse to client interest it can be damaging over a very long period. Tracking is therefore a very important element and tracking against competing issues very valuable. It is at times when the total editorial space universe is contracting that the greatest danger lurks in the fertile mind of the idle journalist. Conversely, if the issue is being promoted, this is the time to give it new and added impetus. The silly season may be an obvious time to promote issues but experience shows that this is not always a time when the greatest exposure, or higher proportion of exposure, can be generated.

Issues compete

An issue can successfully compete with other news. For example, two years prior to Iraq's invasion of Kuwait, a story ran about the controversial supply of arms and industrial equipment. It was interesting to note that this story took editorial space in the same week as the Budget, interest rate cuts, employment figures, inflation and balance of trade news. In the same week major statements were issued by five of the top ten British companies. The *Financial Times* alone was able to devote over a page to the Iraqi shipments story.

The analysts

Unless there is already a very effective system, tracking and evaluating issues in-house is not advisable. There are very good and respectable organisations with a great deal of experience where this can be done confidentially. Such work does require established and trained analysts and, in many cases, if a more appropriate alternative is called for, referrals between such organisations will be offered.

The cost of such tracking is miniscule compared to the value of the data available. It is particularly useful when competitor watching.

Evaluating Press Coverage

In an area as large as corporate public relations, only a fraction of the subjects and issues can be covered in a book such as this. We can expect a great deal more to be said, done and reported over the next months and years. One cannot envisage a future corporate public relations programme which does not look for a measured improvement in press relations and, no doubt, future prize-giving at those institute award ceremonies will be full of charts proving the point.

17

The Effect on Public Relations Practitioners and the Media

There is always a little concern when someone comes along and says they want to measure your work. If the reasons and benefits are explained and a real opportunity to improve professional capability is offered as a result, such assessment is valuable. While there are many ways in which the measures outlined in this book can be misapplied and misused, the potential and overwhelming benefits far outweigh the possible abuses.

More discipline

Media evaluation brings a discipline to the press office where only the best practice will prevail. Poorly kept records, inadequate systems and muddled objectives are quickly exposed. Simple routines such as proper chronology of activity, good record keeping and regular reporting become essential. Analysis will quickly expose administrative inadequacies.

Precise feedback

For those whose job it is to write, and who are already judged by the press from their output, a more precise feedback is provided and acceptance of their words is evident in the records of coverage achieved. This is not just a measure of editorial acceptance but a measure of editors accepting material in preference to others in the same profession. Throughout this book we have assumed the presence of press relations skills. The ability to write effectively and to meet editors' requirements has not been in question. Future measuring will not be based on any assumptions in this area, it will be based on actual performance.

Enhanced media selection

Media selection skills acquired with years of experience are confirmed, enhanced and improved and new skills open up. Here is an opportunity to see some of the great differences between press and public relations and other forms of communication. Those in public relations, whose interests remain rooted primarily in press relations work, will find much of interest in the results of evaluation. Many are now delighting in the new found addition to their expert knowledge.

Proof of good work

More than a few press relations specialists have spent hours defending their work in meetings where marketing and sales managers have been unconvinced about its efficacy. Henceforth, with good monitoring and evaluation, the tables are turned. Articles published, column centimetres, impact measures and statistics to show opportunities to read will be very powerful weapons in such meetings. But it is with those statistics and in the knowledge that the press is exceptionally powerful that the tables are turned. A marketing or sales manager faced with the numbers will have to look at the way he or she regards press coverage afresh. Skilled interpretation of statistics will identify the correctness of a particular press campaign and techniques using data about editorial space universe, competitors' pressures, assumed issue/USP propositions and knowledge-gap satisfaction can be presented for the benefits available.

More believable awards

In time, because press coverage evaluation is growing in stature and usage and in addition to case study material derived from such

Evaluating Press Coverage

Evaluating Press Coverage

Evaluating Press Coverage

events as the Institute of Public Relations awards providing anecdotal statistical evidence, there will be sufficient academic knowledge to show the relative power of press coverage.

Press relations should not be solely judged in promotional terms but measured in terms of behavioural change quotients. This will mean that the public relations manager and consultant will need to understand such matters.

Numerate press officers

The press officer will be dramatically affected by press coverage evaluation in a new area of activity. Numeracy is now going to be important. Identifying what the statistics are really saying will soon be very important. Measuring effectiveness of style and content, identifying press coverage reach, evaluating impact as well as knowing what opportunities coverage is providing to facilitate behavioural change is now a matter of statistical interpretation. And knowing that the figures are correct will also mean the press officer will, in some circumstances, have to stand firm. If the anticipated results are not having the desired effect for the client, it will be no use forsaking the statistics and passing them off with a glib excuse. The press officer will have to tell the client that some other influence is at work – and will have to fight to be heard. If this means a total change to the campaign, so be it. At least the basis for the decision can be made from a position of knowledge rather than gut feel.

Better knowledge of editorial needs

From what we already know, and based on experience to date, the effectiveness of press work comes from dealing with the motivations of editors and readers eager for new information and with enthusiasm for a cause. Press coverage evaluation can be a major contributor in establishing information deficiency, and relevance of issues can track the most probable means to exploit the potential for effective use of press to change behaviour. The new methods of press coverage evaluation show how this will be achieved. Not knowing about such matters will not be an excuse for the future.

A more important role for press cuttings

The advent of services such as press cutting bureaux had a significant effect on the practice of press relations and its measurement in the past. Even so, the presence of cuttings is still too frequently used as some kind of trophy instead of a measurement of effectiveness. This is where evaluation of coverage is going to have the greatest impact on public relations practice.

Compare effectiveness of consultancies

Anyone can now compare the effectiveness of one consultancy with the next, easily and cheaply. Each month the client will want to know how much effective coverage has been achieved and compare this to competition and cost. A lot of public relations executives, in the past able to wind up the wick when the client got upset at the paucity of cuttings, will be found out. In addition those so called consultants unable to show press relations effectiveness in quantifiable terms will find the bigger clients drifting away to more professional organisations.

Measuring public relations activity was once hard. Now it is getting easier for press relations work. The professionals will, of course, enjoy the experience while the less professional will go to the wall.

There are far too many people who call themselves public relations consultants and measured effectiveness will reduce this number. This does not necessarily mean that the big consultancies with the evaluation techniques will be automatically more successful; some will find measurement too hard to swallow and others will have to fight out their methods with better competitors. Equally, specialist press relations organisations will find they can compete on more than equal terms.

The trend for measurement and effective focus in public relations is no longer just a fashionable phase; it has moved on to become a prerequisite and is to be welcomed. We will all change as a result, and for the better.

The effect of evaluation on the media

One of the dangers of press coverage analysis is that it will have an effect on journalists. They will, no doubt, be somewhat affronted that their words and contributions to media can be statistically analysed and evaluated.

Every survey conducted shows that the press corps finds press officers and public relations consultants over-keen to ply irrelevant information. Arming the press office with even tighter goals and objectives and giving them more closely focused objectives will be regarded with horror.

There is well established evidence to suggest that PR impact is sufficiently effective to change the total level of coverage given to a subject, not just in one publication but across a wide swathe of the media. Of course, the only experience we have is from professional consultancies and companies with the confidence to have conducted the research in the first place. Such organisations may well have a different approach to journalists from other less progressive bodies.

One well respected public relations consultant is horrified at the prospect of evaluating coverage in order to work on projections with his clients. His argument is that journalists will resist accepting material for publication, viewing the offering as being 'free' advertising. Such a view is quite valid especially as it comes from a writer whose record in his field, when measured against his peers, is outstanding. He held, for six months, a record as being the most published writer in his chosen subject.

More professionalism from press and PR

It is in his success that the argument fails. His writing is published because it is good, not because he has targets to meet. Journalists not only look forward to receiving his press releases but go out of their way to invite contributions.

As long as the media maintains its healthy disregard for the public relations profession, the impact of evaluation will do nothing but good. But the discipline will affect both practitioner and journalist.

To begin with, the old habit of spraying press releases into the air in order that one copy will land on every editor's desk will be even more discredited. Monitoring quickly shows where there is no interest in a subject and the consultant stops wasting time, effort and money in this futile activity.

Then there are considerations of content and style. Improved monitoring helps the press release writer to present material which is both germane to the publication and in a style matching that of the journal. Editing is easier and the chance of inclusion significantly better.

Effective briefing, when conducted against a background of established attitudes derived from analysis of previous coverage, is helpful in making conversations more valuable to both parties.

Past coverage used in evidence

A good press officer should be able to present a year's coverage given to an industry by a single publication, including benefits gained, a table showing competitor activity and details about usage of photographs etc. When the journalist finds out that prejudices have become well known, there may be some interesting exchanges and this may not be such a bad thing.

On the other hand some of the information available to journalists through media measurement may be both useful and disquieting.

Quantify bias

Using effectiveness monitoring, it is already quite easy to quantify bias in both reporting and coverage. No doubt politicians and others will be in a position to prove such points in the near future and publications will equally be able to assess how well balanced their coverage is, using the same methods. There is at least one magazine which compares the coverage it gives to different companies in an effort to be even-handed between them. Such practice is a major problem for the consultant in that excellence has no chance to shine. One may also be critical of such a publication on the grounds that it is insensitive to differences between competitors.

Identify the unworthy publications

There is reason to believe the press is not always as efficacious as it would like to believe. Already, tracking shows that the effectiveness of some editorial in changing both attitudes and, it follows, behaviour is not as significant in some journals as the editors believe. This may have something to do with the sheer numbers of publications available or the confusion in editorial stance obvious in some publications with a different approach to issues in different sections of the publication. At present monitoring is not providing concrete answers. It is showing that in areas where high volumes of coverage are achieved, different publications have a specific role in the wider acceptance of a story or issue. While this may be a further case for more focused press relations, identifying how to achieve such focus to progress a story is not as apparent as first impressions would indicate.

Parallel advertising measures

Over the next few years, as press coverage evaluation becomes more widely used, an additional rating of the effectiveness of journals will emerge to work in parallel as an added test of advertising measures.

Many consultancies have been following a policy of close targeting with highly focused campaigns but have not found the resulting media impact acceptable. In a number of cases, direct marketing techniques have been found to be significantly more effective than newspapers and journals. We shall have to wait and see, but some publications might have to review their editorial policies when research from monitoring editorial coverage is added to the marketing mix.

Context monitor used for advertising policy

It was an article in a very popular newspaper which first illustrated the impact that editorial coverage can have on advertising policy. The newspaper published a story about a company's redundancies. Tracking over a number of months confirmed that the newspaper predominantly reported bad news about industry in general, industrial accidents in particular, and had a marked reluctance to cover innovation, excellence and good management practice. Against this background it was considered that advertising a particular product which could have reached a high proportion of the required market/readership would, nevertheless, be contextually disadvantaged in this medium.

Advertisers judge their media on a variety of traditional criteria but seldom on the well-researched contextual effect of an advertisement in a publication whose editorial stance could detract from marketing effectiveness. Until recently, statistics covering the effect of editorial context were not sufficiently well proven and advertisers made judgements on relatively flimsy evidence. Today's more quantifiable data will aid their future choice.

Plagiarism monitor

There is a case for monitoring some publications and broadcasts which are effective as opinion leaders for the rest of the media. This allows the press office to catch issues as they emerge. Journalists will find this very irritating because it will significantly affect their news sources.

The following example is taken from the BBC television programme *Panorama*: it proves that the ability to track sources for information can highlight some of the more glaring errors in reporting.

A *Panorama* programme was investigating the support a company received for its export activities and, in the interview, identified the British Overseas Trade Board (BOTB) as being of particular help. The reporter then announced that the Department of Trade and Industry (DTI) had no direct knowledge of the help given. Having identified the two sources mentioned it was obvious that the question was asked of the wrong institution as BOTB operates at a distance from the DTI. The slant this gave to the story was wholly contrary to the facts. If this had been a newspaper report such errors would have been quickly identified. Continuous tracking would thereafter monitor similar inaccuracies in the same and disparate media. In the quoted incident, the press did follow up the story but did not verify the facts. The effectiveness of *Panorama* as a leading source for news reporters was quite evident and remedial action required frantic activity to redress perceptions. Tracking the story showed how effective the press relations campaign had been, but had tracking been available for television the remedy would have been faster and more effective and less damage would have been done.

Knowing what to watch

Most publications track issues as a means of identifying the popularity of subjects among other journals. Using modern media-tracking methods this can become a very effective way of identifying the relative importance of different stories. There is no evidence of this kind of tracking being done scientifically but it is an obvious route for editors to follow in due course. A case of gamekeeper watching gamekeeper.

The existence of major electronic libraries of information and the type of analysis we have considered in this book, means that effective press and public relations work will change. In the case where inaccuracy in a story is identified in one of these databanks, a press officer will be able to introduce a corrective element by seeking coverage in publications on the same database and so affect the background material available to journalists. While, in time, this will mean that some journalists will be sceptical of some of the background and will revert to a more investigative style, the majority will follow the current BBC philosophy and do the desk research first. There are more than a few cases of stories being over-exposed on an unreliable premise and without sufficient corrective information to redress the issue.

There is little comfort for any but the most professional in the press as public relations practitioners measure the work of journalists with a more critical eye. Based on careful, detailed and often statistical precision, public relations and press office experts will be just that – critical. The public relations profession is improving its press relations capability and will come to expect a different attitude from the media. Equally the media can look forward to improved professionalism from public relations people with very direct and more highly focused objectives in view.

Conclusions

Evaluating press relations can be simple or complex according to your needs. This book has shown some of the simplest methods and has covered many issues which can complicate coverage assessment.

In the vast majority of cases, the measures required for press relations campaigns can be simple. There is little need for complexity. With many campaigns, beyond simple measures of comparable competence and cost effectiveness there need be little to add to measurement further than reading the cuttings with care.

Experience proves that eventually such tracking inspires the client to achieve greater command in the media and even more precise analysis of impact.

Progressively this will take the whole business of press coverage analysis into yet more complex areas and clients will be looking for the kind of quantifiable measure achieved in other management fields. The measures will not be the same though; clients will be looking for powerful indications of behavioural change which will be distinctive and different from the kind of presence achieved through other promotions.

European measurement

The worldwide issue of measured press relations has so far only been touched upon. In the USA, detailed analysis is becoming almost commonplace. In Europe it is unusual and, outside the UK, not wholly practical for a number of reasons. Simple problems still exist such as the inadequacy of press cutting bureaux and lack of electronic data about the press. This will all be overcome within a

Conclusions

few years and press coverage evaluation will be available across the European Community and the rest of Europe in months rather than years.

The ability to judge press campaigns across Europe will be of enormous benefit to those companies looking for measured pan-Europe presence.

Radio and television

There are still questions to be raised about assessing the impact of radio and television.

While there is considerable research going into providing evaluation services in this area, experience is thin on the ground. The need is considerable and such services will be popular. Fortunately, as a direct result of research into violence on television in the USA, we are already aware of many of the techniques required to evaluate television coverage and so the development of effective systems cannot be far off.

Measurement agencies

The rising popularity of press coverage evaluation is most remarkable; while research has been conducted by a range of companies and consultancies for many years, it is only in the last two or three that systems have been developed and brought into common use. Furthermore, in the first three months of 1991 three new systems were being independently developed and more are in the pipeline.

So far, only these three systems are generally available to all press and public relations practitioners, the remainder being prepared by consultancies for their own use to add value to the press relations products offered to clients. In 1991 these amounted to seven additional systems in the UK.

Why wait until now

On discovering the many benefits available from press coverage analysis one is tempted to ask why this kind of service has not been generally available before. The reasons are manifold: the public relations profession believed its success was sufficiently obvious, especially when measured against ever rising fee turnover. Further measurements of excellence were not needed. At the same time many practitioners were coming to the conclusion that press relations work was a diminishing component of public relations. This was especially true, since other areas in corporate, political and financial relations were bigger fee earners.

There was also some doubt about how effective press coverage could be compared to highly targeted one-on-one briefing. The concept of laser focus on an opinion forming clique counted in hundreds rather than the massed millions of press readership gained considerable sway. That was until the media took a different view and began to interfere in these cosy discussions. At the same time it became evident that tertiary opinion forming, especially via the media, is still a very potent part of the mix. The press in particular began to champion causes, many of which mobilised public opinion in a way more powerful than before. Targeted briefing on green issues, political upheaval in Eastern Europe, the economy, the Gulf War and other areas became not just public issues but had profound impact on the corporate state and industry.

With the onset of the recession a number of public relations activities became much less profitable or simply stopped. The rush of mergers and acquisitions turned into an avalanche of redundancies and closures. At the same time hard pressed clients wanted proof of effectiveness for bread and butter press relations activity and without adequate evidence of both success and effectiveness, cut budgets. There was an urgent need to find a system by which to identify the impact of press relations.

And so a revolutionary change took place; it will be popular and even fashionable before settling down as a normal and ordinary part of professional public relations practice.

There will be extraordinary claims for the effectiveness of press measurement before then, together with much use, abuse and experimentation. Inexorably, this process will demand a higher level of professionalism among clients and public relations practitioners.

Informed and improved quality

An improvement in the quality of the relationship between press officers and journalists is well overdue. Measuring press efficacy is

Conclusions

a two way street and for a long time journalists have been proved as effective as the revenues their publications attract. From now on a body of informed opinion will be able to judge the media in a different light.

Postscript

Throughout the preparation of this book, the author has been helped by many examples drawn from public relations experts and from a wide range of press relations managers. In addition many of the examples of methodology have been taken from Press Relations Performance Review, a press coverage evaluation system provided by Media Measurement Limited, where the author is a director.

Media Measurement Limited was formed in 1991 to bring a system of press coverage evaluation into common usage. Its first product was called Press Relations Performance Review. Purposely designed to be a standard product yet reasonably flexible it is priced at a cost acceptable to the majority of press relations programmes. It is by no means the most sophisticated system nor is it possible to change the structure of the measures involved.

Press Relations Performance Review is a computer-based system using key words and phrases, cuttings and a comprehensive database of information about British publications.

With information supplied by customers on a standard form, analysts process the data and return a report and the cuttings in a few days. Much of the jargon used here is derived from this system and so will not come as a great surprise! Within certain parameters customers specify a unique pattern for evaluation comprising:

Principal key word

The principal key word/phrase/issue up to 25 characters long. This can be, for example, a company name or a type of product or an issue. Usually it coincides with the same brief given to the cutting bureaux.

Postscript

The customer can add up to five other key words, called secondary key words (SKW) which are always related to the principal key word. Whenever this word is found, it will always be attributed to the principal key word (PKW).

This is useful to see coverage about a product or subject compared with the overall picture about the principal key word.

Other notable words

Customers choose up to five other notable words (ONW), which will be looked for at the same time. Once again they can be up to 25 characters long. These might be competitors or other subjects, issues or phrases. For example, this may include a competitor's product or the name of a competitor's managing director.

Key publications

Another facility is to identify up to ten publications which are key, target journals. These are split into two sections to allow definition of coverage in two different groups of five. Press Relations Performance Review will identify these publications in a special report whenever coverage is received in these journals.

There are three written reports:

Press cutting analysis

For each press cutting a report is generated attributing coverage to the key words and:

- journal name, address, editor, circulation, frequency, Romieke & Curties classification;
- beneficial, neutral and adverse attribution of column centimetres, photograph and headline (if a reference is made);
- a third-party source and/or journalists' byline;
- enquiry opportunities such as address or enquiry reference number;
- reference number, date completed, and the name of the analyst.

In addition a record of past coverage, if any, is included with a similar analysis.

Executive analysis

Each month, or when reports are called off, an executive review is generated. This includes details of the base for analysis, total articles, ccm, occurrence of articles on f/c, name in headline and photograph.

A beneficial, neutral and adverse rating is included as are the total opportunities to read (cumulative circulation).

A list of third-party sources and journalist bylines is also generated and a comparable report on the other notable words (frequently competitors) is included.

Detailed report

For more detailed analysis a monthly report is also provided which covers cutting evaluation in the following terms:

- this month and historic;
- beneficial, neutral and adverse;
- ccm;
- actual, average and graphical statistics;
- ratios;
- most frequent publications;
- target journal coverage and circulation 'opportunities to read';
- most reported bylines;
- most reported sources.

Press Relations Performance Review is designed to provide a wide range of management information. More than just a record of success, it provides comparative information and identifies unusual types of coverage. The tracking capability allows issues to be followed and progressive improvement in coverage as a campaign proceeds. The circulation figures show what opportunities to read have been generated and the success level in the most important publications. With the record of coverage maintained and kept up to date, press lists can be verified while listings of bylined journalists and third-party information sources also provide ready made reference lists for future use.

For issue management, the ability to see how issues are covered and to what depth, as well as by whom, is extremely useful. The

Postscript

system of BNA used is of the 'directly attributable to key word' type. In addition, the total editorial universe for a given subject can be obtained from this analysis.

Appendix 1

Press Cutting Specification

a) Single Key Word

Contact name ....
Position...
Company name..
Address...
....
....
Postcode...
Telephone number ....
Fax number...
Order number ....
Address for cuttings (if different from above)..............
....
....
Postcode...
Name and address for invoice (if different from above) ....
....
....
....
Postcode...
Cutting analysis to commence on (date) ....
and for 12 months or until further notice thereafter.
Analysis will be made for the following key word definition:...........

Appendix 1

(this can be a company or organisation name or a generic, such as vacuum cleaner, or it can be an issue)

....

Sometimes known as:
(this can be an acronym, abbreviation or commonly used alternative, such as a brand name)

....

Type of business or activity:
(this will be a description of the business or activity of the key word)

....

What the product/service is/does:
(this description sets the key word in context and can be quite broad in scope)

....

Associated names or products always associated with the key word:
(this may include product or unique product definition always associated with the key word)

....

Exclusions:
(this may indicate divisions of the company to be excluded and the associated products or activities or similar exclusions for other types of organisation)

....

Anticipated publications:

- Type..
- Frequency ....
- Typical example ....
- Predominantly national ....

Evaluating Press Coverage

- Regional..
- Business ....
- Consumer..
- Women's interest ....
- Special interest...
- Trade and technical ....
- Other ....

Media exclusions (if any):

- Type (eg trade and technical)...
- Typical example ....

Type of cutting required:

- Full page when appearance occurs..
- Page number and total pages...
- Regular delivery...
- Fast delivery...
- Rush delivery..

Please include circulation of the publication for each cutting.

Appendix 1

b) Multi Key Word

In many instances there is a requirement to cut for more than one key word – for a whole industry or area of interest. In such a case in addition to the single key word specification the following will be useful to add:

Principal key word (replaces 'key word definition' in the single key word specification):
(this can be an industry, or organisation group name or an interest area or it can be an issue)
....

Key word two:..
Sometimes known as: ....
Business or activity:...
Product/service: ....
Associated names/products always associated:.....................................

Exclusions:
(this may indicate divisions of the company to be excluded and the associated products or activities or similar exclusions for other types of organisation)
....

Additional key words can be included by repeating these instructions.

Appendix 2

Subcontractor/Consultancy Agreement

Introduction

This Agreement has been prepared to ensure that, from the commencement of the Subcontractor/Consultancy relationship, each party fully understands its respective rights, duties and procedures.

This agreement is between the two parties as contractors to ....
....
hereinafter referred to as 'the Client'.

The Subcontractor will cooperate fully with the Consultancy in the planning and execution of a press relations programme to be agreed between the parties. The Consultancy agrees to assist the Subcontractor in the performance of these duties by making available to the Subcontractor all relevant information which shall include:

Background and detailed briefing about the Client, including details of facilities, products, financial information relevant to the press, product information and details about manufacturing processes, distribution and after sales support as are necessary to the execution of the press relations work for the Client.

New products to be launched on territory, news of relevant major orders, newsworthy technical information and applications about products in other territories as are necessary in the execution of the press relations work for the Client.

Subcontractor Status

The Subcontractor acts in all its contracts as a principal at law.

Appendix 2

Exclusivity

The Subcontractor will not represent conflicting or competing interests without prior agreement by the Consultancy, who will also advise the Subcontractor of any intention to engage additional subcontractor services other than those already advised.

Clause 1	**Appointment and Programme**
	This agreement confirms the appointment of
	....
	(hereinafter referred to as 'the Subcontractor)
	as Public Relations Consultants to
	[a Company]
	....
	(hereinafter referred to as 'the Consultancy')
	to carry out a press relations programme, details of which are attached and initialled by the parties for identification.
Clause 2	**Commencement and Duration of the Agreement**
	This appointment will commence on
	....
	and will continue in effect unless terminated under the provisions of Clause 10 of this agreement.
Clause 3	**Fees**
	The Subcontractor's fees, exclusive of VAT, and based on press coverage achieved as agreed in the press relations programme agreed and attached and initialled by both parties as aforementioned, will be calculated at the rate of:
	Per article published £.......
	Per column cm published £.......
	Provided that such articles and such column centimetres:

Evaluating Press Coverage

(i) appear in those journals identified in the press relations programme aforementioned;

(ii) such articles will include the key words as agreed in the programme aforementioned

Always providing that such remuneration shall not exceed more than £......... in one calendar month.

...................................(payable monthly in arrears)

The Subcontractor reserves the right to negotiate a revised fee structure should changes in the agreed press coverage take place during the term of this agreement.

These fees apply to work carried out only in ....(country) (herein call 'the Territory') and do not apply to work performed in any other country which will be subject to separate fee arrangements.

| Clause 4 | **Disbursements and Expenses** |

(a) The Subcontractor fee shall be exclusive of the following disbursements and expense items relating to the agreed programme:

- advertising artwork and mechanical items (ie blocks, typesetting);
- exhibition and display material;
- film production design, artwork and printing;
- market research;
- media monitoring (radio, television and press);
- messenger services;
- photography and prints;
- special events, meetings, conferences, etc.

The Consultancy agrees to pay immediately upon presentation any interim invoices in respect of advance or instalment payments required to be made to suppliers.

Appendix 2

Clause 5	**Payment Terms**

The Subcontractor's fees are payable monthly to reach the subcontractor not later than 30 days after the invoice date.

Disbursement and expenses invoices are payable within 30 days of the date on which they are rendered.

Clause 6	**Approvals and Authority**

The Subcontractor will affect the provisions of the programme and will report to the consultancy completion of each element of the programme as it is achieved and as provided for in the programme.

The Subcontractor will make such arrangements as necessary to collect all press mentions and related text which includes such trade names, product nomenclature and other statements relating to the client as are agreed in the programme.

The Subcontactor shall provide copies of such press mentions to the Consultancy together with the name of the journal, date of publication, reference to the specific press release or briefing provided to the journal, the photographic reference number, column centimetres in length and reference to such key word and nomenclature as are provided and in such time as provided for in the programme.

After obtaining general approval of campaign or project plans the Subcontractor will submit to the Consultancy for approval from the Client's appointed representative on territory and to the Consultancy for specific approval:

(i) draft press releases, articles, photographs and captions;

(ii) copy, layouts, artwork and/or scripts.

A copy of all press releases and the circulation to journals for such press releases, together with reports of conversations with journalists about the Client in any and all its forms shall be provided to the Consultancy forthwith.

The Subcontractor shall not defame, criticise or otherwise bring the Client of the Consultancy into disrepute.

Evaluating Press Coverage

The Subcontractor shall identify any article or commentary which is defamatory, adversely critical or which brings the client of the Consultancy into disrepute.

The Sub-contractor shall take such articles as are provided about the client, its products and services, contracts, photographs and other material which can be used to gain added press coverage for the client on territory and in addition will attend such places in the territory as shall provide case study or application press stories to enhance the repute of the client, products or services and write and present such stories for publication in the trade, technical and other appropriate press as provided for in the programme and within the conventions professionally acceptable by the association affiliated to International Committee of Public Relations Consultancies Association (ICO) and Confederation Europeanne des Relations Publiques (CERP) on territory.

The Subcontractor shall not remit any payment to the consultancy for placing any article in any journal.

The Subcontractor shall take all necessary steps required to provide such visits as are required on territory for journalists to visit facilities on territory and overseas and to accept inward missions of journalists as provided for in the programme within the fee agreed.

Written approval by the Consultancy of the drafts and proofs will be taken by the Subcontractor as authorization to proceed to publication and such approval will be taken as authorization to enter into contracts with suppliers on the basis of those estimates.

The Subcontractor will take all reasonable steps to comply with any requests from the Consultancy to amend or halt any plans or to reject or cancel any work in the process of preparation, in so far as this is possible within the scope of its contractual obligations to its suppliers.

Any amendment or cancellation will be implemented by the Subcontractor.

Appendix 2

Clause 7	**Copyright**
	The copyright of all artwork, copy and other work produced by the Subcontractor rests AT ALL TIMES WITH THE CONSULTANCY.
Clause 8	**Confidential Information**
	The Subcontractor acknowledges a duty not to disclose without Consultancy or Client permission during or after its term of appointment any confidential information resulting from studies or surveys commissioned and paid for by the Consultancy. The Client and Consultancy in turn acknowledges the Subcontractor's right to use as it sees fit any general intelligence regarding Consultancy products or services which it has gained in the course of its appointment.
Clause 9	**Insurance**
	(a) **Professional Indemnity**
	The Consultancy shall indemnify and keep indemnified the Subcontractor from and against any and all proceedings, claims, damages, losses, expenses or liabilities which the Subcontractor may incur or sustain as a direct or indirect result of or in connection with any information, representation, reports, data or material supplied, prepared or specifically approved (as described in paragraph I of Clause 6) by the Consultancy particularly in relation to proceedings under the Trade Descriptions Act 1968 and such akin legislation for the time being in force in the territory. Such material to include press releases, articles, copy, scripts, artwork and detailed plans or programmes.
	(b) **Consultancy's Property**
	Any property or information made available by the Consultancy to the Subcontractor for the purposes of demonstration or publicity or for any other purpose arising from or in connection with this agreement shall be and at all times remain at the sole and entire risk of the Consultancy, and the Subcontractor shall not be subject to any liability for it.

Clause 10	**Termination Provisions**
	This agreement may be terminated at any time after an initial period of .... months by either party giving not less than ...... months' written notice of termination to the other.
	In the event of termination of this agreement for whatever reason, the Consultancy will be responsible for all fees payable hereunder to the Subcontractor and costs, expenses and disbursements incurred by the Subcontractor on behalf of the Consultancy up to and including any notice period.
	On the satisfaction by the Consultancy in full of its payment obligations, the Subcontractor will co-operate with the Consultancy so far as practicable in enabling the Consultancy to take over any contract and arrangement with third parties, and will transfer to the Consultancy any unused materials purchased on behalf of the Consultancy.
	The parties will agree as to any additional compensation payable to the Subcontractor in the event that detailed creative or other work for a future programme or project prepared by the Subcontractor at the request of the Consultancy during the period of this Agreement is subsequently implemented in whole or in part by or on behalf of the Consultancy.
Clause 11	Contract Agreement
	For and on behalf of
	[a Company]
	....
	(Name of Subcontractor)
	Date..
	Signature...
	For and on behalf of..
	....

Appendix 2

(Name of Consultancy)

Date..

Signature...

NOTES

Note 1	The Subcontractor should note the need for clear agreement on terms when payment in foreign currency or when rates of exchange ruling at any given time is involved.
Note 2	Two fundamental principles on which the Subcontractor/Consultancy financial relationship is based are:
	(i) The Subcontractor shall finance its own operations but not costs incurred on behalf of its Consultancy.
	(ii) As principal at law, the Subcontractor is held by suppliers as solely liable for payment.
Note 3	The language for all commercial transactions under this agreement shall be English.
	All material to be provided for the press will be written in the language commonly used in the territory where it is written.

Appendix 3

A Press Coverage Analysis

SUMMARY OF PRESS COVERAGE – MARCH 1991

Executive Summary

Overall coverage has been higher than normal for this time of the year, continuing the upward trend. Excellent coverage was achieved in the *Financial Times*, and *The Grocer* ran a favourable comment on our policy – a marked change from previous reports. Good showings were also seen in key features – in each case far more effectively than the main competitors.

Appendix 3

OUTPUT

JANUARY

Press Releases:

Subject	Date sent	Sent to	Published in	%Success rate
New contract	Jan 2	42 titles	38	72
Industry comment	Jan 12	12 titles	8	64

Features:

Subject	Sent to	Published/Date
Case study	Grocer	Yes – Jan 15
Technical article	Super Marketing	Yes – Jan 8

FEBRUARY

Etc.

Evaluating Press Coverage

SUMMARY OF OUTPUT PRESS RELEASES

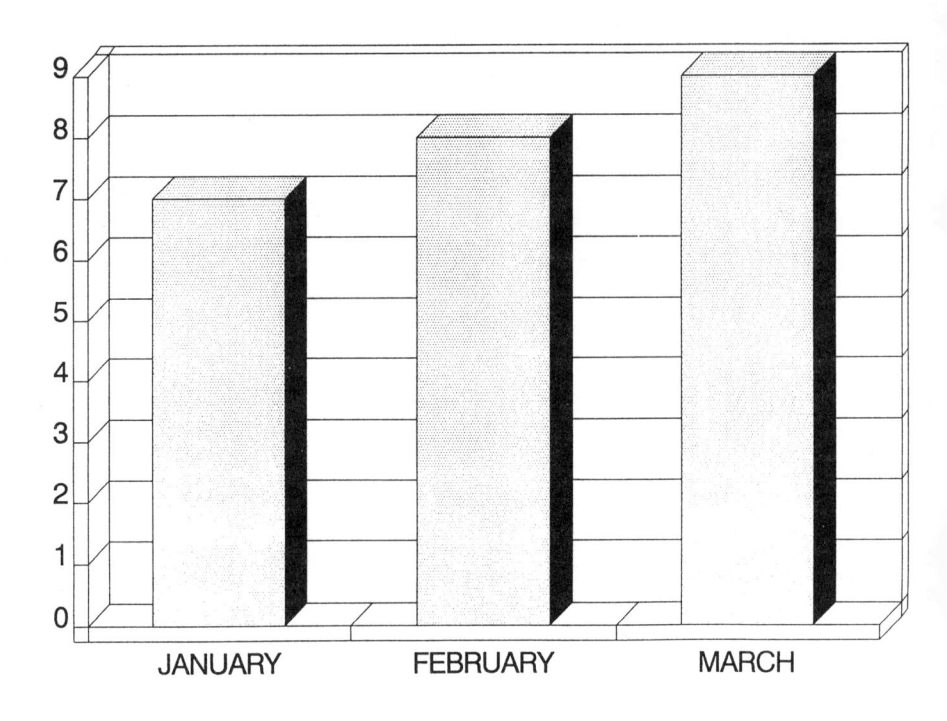

	JANUARY	FEBRUARY	MARCH
Press Releases	7	8	9

Appendix 3

SUMMARY OF OUTPUT FEATURES

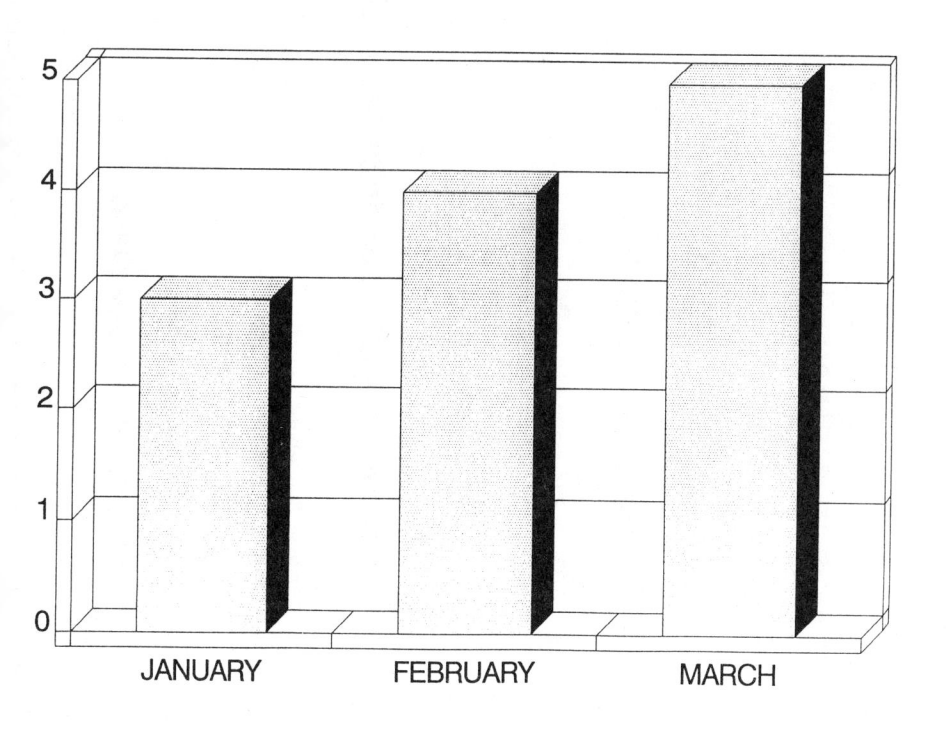

Evaluating Press Coverage

COMBINED OUTPUT

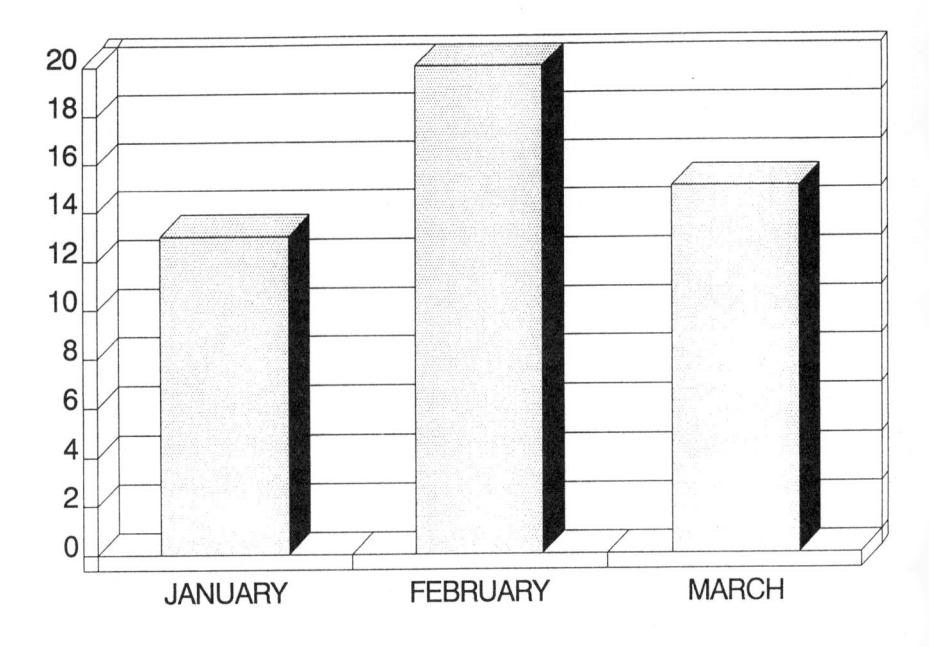

Appendix 3

COVERAGE – PRESS RELEASES

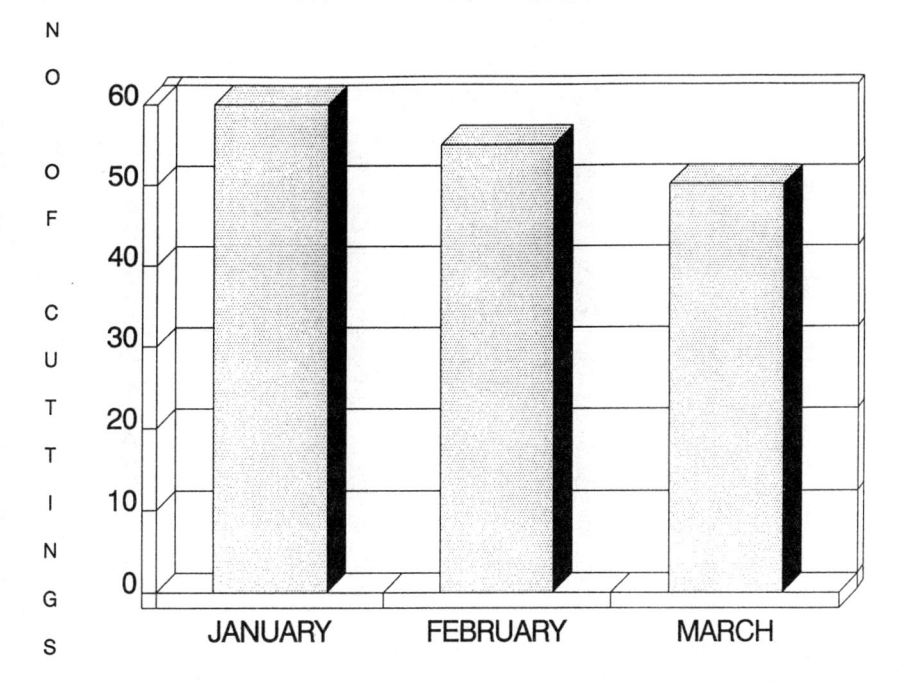

NO OF CUTTINGS

	JANUARY	FEBRUARY	MARCH

COVERAGE – FEATURES

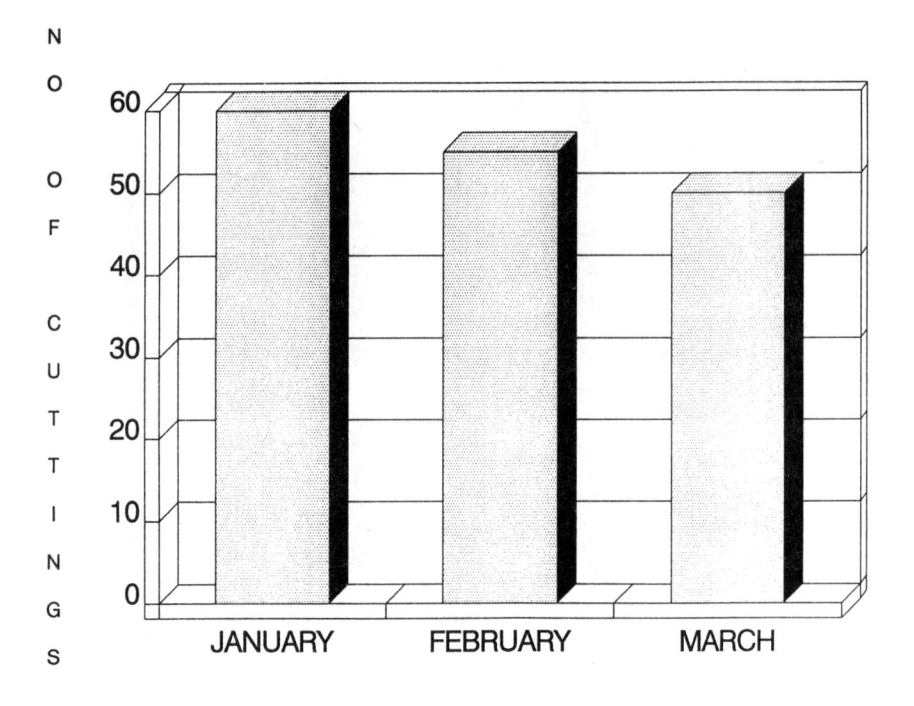

N
O
O
F
C
U
T
T
I
N
G
S

| | JANUARY | FEBRUARY | MARCH |

Appendix 3

COVERAGE -V- OUTPUT

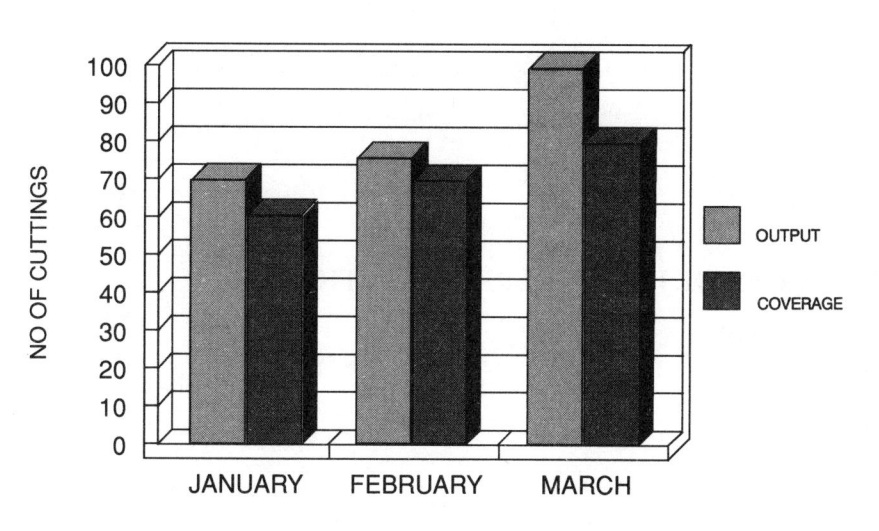

COVERAGE AS % OF OUTPUT

January	18%
February	28%
March	8%

NAMES OF JOURNALISTS MENTIONED
JANUARY

Write	Position	Journal	Subject
John Smith	Editor	Building Week	Nuts
Fred Bloggs	Cookery Editor	Good Food	French Wine

FEBRUARY
Etc.

Appendix 3

COVERAGE IN KEY JOURNALS

Journal	January	February	March
Grocer	0	1	1
Super Marketing	1	0	0
Financial Times	0	0	1
Telegraph	1	2	3
etc			
etc			
etc			
etc			
etc			

NUMBER OF CUTTINGS PER CATEGORY

	JANUARY	FEBRUARY	MARCH
Nationals	30	20	18
Primary Trade	50	62	79
Regional Business & Secondary Trade	8	7	14
Local Press	2	93	1
Broadcast Media	2	0	1

Appendix 3

MESSAGES CONVEYED

% OF CUTTINGS

	JANUARY	FEBRUARY	MARCH
International capability	68	72	98
Blue chip client base	95	60	40
Benefits of third party	10	90	98
Total supply chain management capability	15	2	1
Industry leadership	22	43	72
Users of sophisticated information technology	9	1	2

Evaluating Press Coverage

COMPARISON WITH COMPETITOR COVERAGE

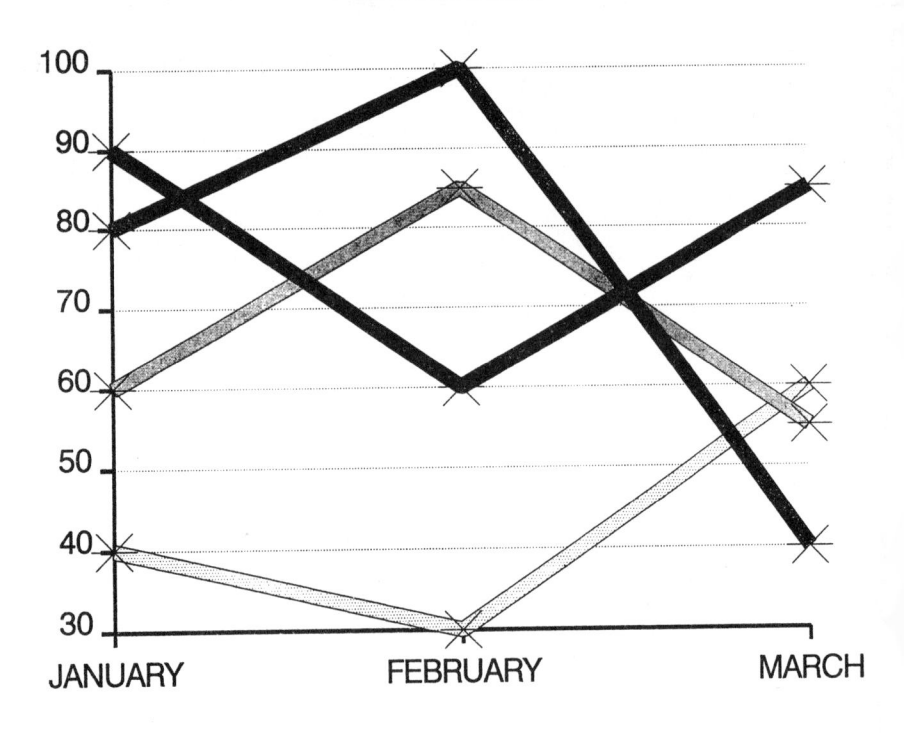

Appendix 3

USE OF PHOTOGRAPHY

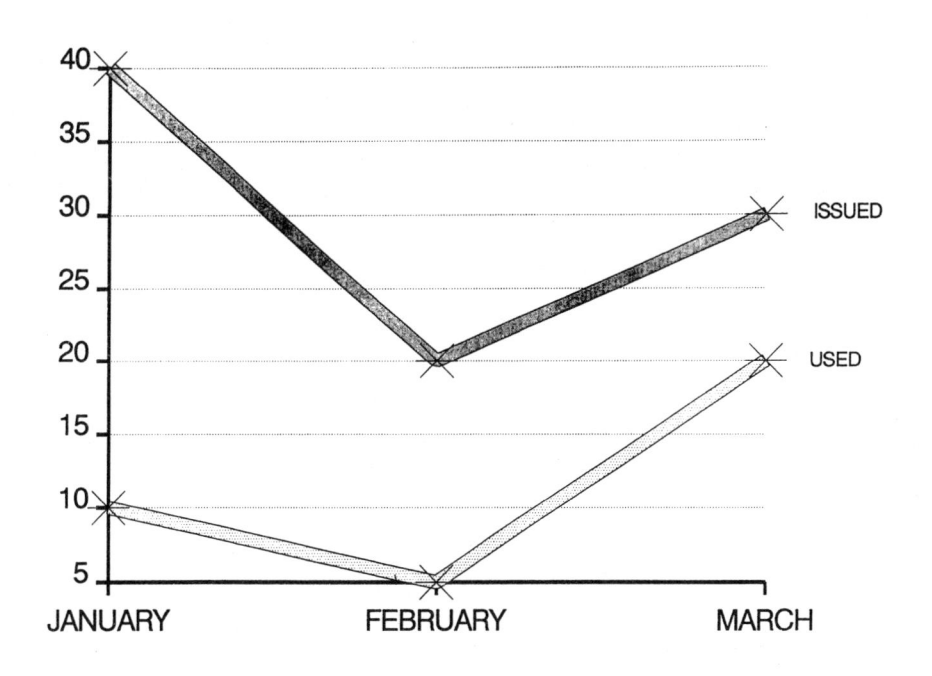

	JANUARY	FEBRUARY	MARCH
ISSUED	40	20	30
USED	10	5	20

231

INDEX

Note: Page numbers in **bold** type indicate material in Figures; those in *italic* type denote textual references to information given in Figures.

ABC ratings 136
acceptability 105–7, 115
acceptance 35–6, 38, 96, 98
accountability 85
accuracy 21, 54, 128
acronyms 24, 100, 207
Adedeji, A **91**
Advance 131
adverse rating, *see* BNA
advertising 62, 78, 138, 154, 167, 169
  avoiding confusion with 48
  campaigns 95, 128, 158, 164
  costs 145
  editorial and 65, 79, 159, 162, 172;
    perceived in different lights **43**
  effect and impact 68
  free 193
  measuring cover against *44*, **46**
  monitoring as 143-8
  more powerful than 72–3
  parallel measures 195
  revenue 121
  sales effort 63
  space 146
  timing and message achieved through 115
  value 147

'advertorials' 79
AID measures 128
ambivalence 97, 98
American Express 85–8, 92
analysis 127, 128, 132, 186, 205, 218–31
  audience 93, 94, 151, 157
  by area 136–8
  comparative 104
  context *44*
  contract 42
  cuttings 86, 116, 144, 203
  dangers 193
  database 141
  detailed 198
  early criteria 187
  editorial 169
  executive 204
  historical 104–7
  impact 198
  initial cost of setting up 182
  many benefits available from 199
  more closely focused 185
  political 176, 178, 179
  postcode type 136–7
  predictive 183
  press relations, for the

marketeer 120
publications 59, **60**
regional 177
selective 176
source 177
statistical 176
subsequent 166
valuable 147
wide 176
see also content analysis
analysts 187–8
Andriessen, F **91**
appearances 59, 96, **105, 106, 108,** 153
archiving 31, 56
Argentina 179
Arthur Anderson & Co **91**
articles 59, 80, 86, 87, 100, 138
 adverse 119
 ascribing values to measures *51, 52*
 average, per press release **38,** *40,* **109**
 bad, value of 147–8
 beneficial, exclusive and long 109
 composite productions 78, 84
 count of 61
 exploratory 71
 influence 96
 length 47
  average **39,** *40,* 105, 155
 main 83
 number of *105,* 112, 123, 124, 155
 occurrence of 204
 penetration in **142**
 percentage of cover 144–5
 published **32,** *62,* **112, 114,** 190
 qualitative judgement on 99
 size **114,** 144
  and circulation growth 126
  relative 169
  significance of *42,* **43**
 surrounding 44
 total **53,** 204
 unsolicited **62,** *63*

variation of effectiveness 147–8
word counts *33,* **34**
assessment 22, *51,* **53,** 149-51, 178–9
 distorted 94
 impact **50,** 82, *53,* 119
AT&T 19
attitudes 69, **88,** *89,* 102, 130, 165
 established 194
 failure to change 73
 forecasting 95–6
 identifying 186
 impact on 72
 interpretation 94
 journalists' 41, 84–5
 measuring, to plan campaigns 99
 monitoring 180
 predicting 92
 see also attitudinal change;
 behaviour; behavioural change
attitudinal change 68, 76, 83, 138, 161, 195
 complete 110
 coverage and 160
 editorial 125
 identifying 85
 media 180
 motivation behind 73
 probable 96
 tracking 84, 97
attribution 78–100, 171
 direct, to key word 93, 205
 inferred 81
 principal/secondary 81
 validity at the time of 83–4
audiences 64, 103, 166
 analysis 93, 151, 157
 briefing 94–5
 definition of 165
 different 100, 160
 educated and articulate 164
 knowledge 100, 165
  accrued advantages 146
 mass 164
 perception 82, 92–3, 97, 100
  and attitudes 95

234

Index

pervasiveness across 151
reaching 54, 130, 131, 168
relevant/required 145, 150, 151
research 59, 100
target **137**, 167
wide, expressing complex ideas to 162
awards 190–1

Barr (A J) & Company 19, 85
behaviour 68, 159, 160
   measuring effect of editorial on 75–6
   media 18
   voting 73–5
behavioural change 73, 77, 159, 191, 195
   motivation behind 75, 110
   powerful indications of 198
   targeting 95
below-the-line activity 138, 149, 154, 158
beneficial rating, *see* BNA
bias 179, 194
BNA (beneficial, neutral and adverse) coverage 110, 132, 146, 171, 183, 204
   attribution 82–4, 94, 97, 203, 205
   campaign planning and 152, 153
Boss Trucks Limited **142**
brand names 79, 183, 207
brand-specific attributes 86, 87
briefings 24–6, 38, 87
   assignment of 59
   audience 94–5
   effective 194
   elementary performance-related 153–4
   highly targeted one-in-one 200
British Embassy 180
British Overseas Trade Board 196
Brittan, Leon **91**
broadcasts 196
Bush, George 80, 81, 82, 83, **91**
buying habits 160

by-lines 41, 58, 84, 204

CACI Marketing Analysis 137
campaigns 54, 87, 119, 168, 179, 198
   advertising 95, 128, 158, 164
   below-the-line 158
   distribution 134
   effective 123, 196
   election 178
   fixed-cost 170
   future 94, 125
   highly focused 195
   impact 151
   management 178
   no impact 41
   objectives 59, 79, 97, 165–6
   narrow 163
   performance-related 173
   planning 53, 84, 99, 127–8, 140, 149–58
   future 94, 125
   impact on 107
   promotional 105, 157
   public relations 83, 93
   regional 135–8
   response-oriented 76
   specific 127
   tracking record over a number of 115
CARMA (Computer-aided Research and Media Analysis) International 19, 85–92
case studies
   campaign planning 157–8
   effectiveness 163, 166–7
   international press programmes 170, 172
   monitoring output 65–6
   tracking 115, 117–18
ccm (column centimetres) 33–6, 65, 143–4, 147, 171, 190, 204
   article length **39**, 47
   attribution and 61, 81, 82, 95
   cuttings and 40, 114
   enquiries received **62**, *63*

235

industry coverage in **39**, **101**, **106**, **108**, **118**, **121**
number of mentions and 172
predicting coverage as 124
press relations campaign in 154
published **38**, *40*, **113**, **114**
rating 48
share of 64
targets to be achieved in 153
charts 31-2, 39-40, 86-7, 115, 117-18, 188
achievement 136
graphs and *142*
Chevellard, G **91**
circulation 33, 96, 102, 115, 123, 203
area 136
assessing 22
cumulative 204
exposure 161
figures 128-30, 138
growth 126
identifying 80
lists 26
mass 134
newspaper 137, 160
reach 71, 130, 161, 164, 176
column inches **32**
see also ccm
Combes, Maxwell E 18
communications 100, 164, 167, 190
mass 135
Communist regimes 89
competition/competitors 23, 87, 116-18, 122-3, 131-2, 144, 154, 166, 192
activity 194
adverse contribution to effectiveness 65
assessing strength 149-50
campaign measured against 51
companies 81
comparison with 230
contract analysis and 42
coverage 41
cuttings for client and *116*, **117**

differences between 194
distorted assessment between company and 94
identifying success of 40
impact of 152
important/relevant 22
and issues 103
leading 163
main 218
not enough time to follow activities of 86
overview 153
pressures 190
previous 161
principal **52**
products of 167, 203
research across all 76
share of coverage against all 64
share of ESU between 182
significant edge over 99
subsidiary company coverage and 184
tracking 104, 138, 181
yardstick 101-10
computers 137, 140-2, 145, 160, 182
analytical systems 185, 202
see also CARMA; data; databases; electronic libraries; software
Conference on Issues and Media 19, 28, 160
consumer demand 160
content 38, 138, 147
decisions on 84
eye-catching 44
reader's regard for 101
style and 59-61, 73, 75, 104, 191, 194
content analysis 41-2, 66, 90, 92, 96, 159
detailed 79, 86
disadvantages 160
in USA 18-19
context 93, 95, 100, 195-6
analysis 44

Index

editorial 196
  key words in 44, **45**
contracts 42, 173, 174
contribution 96, 97, 98
copyright 173
corporate image 86, 107, 119, 183
correspondents 84
costs 104, 145, 158, 160, 170, 192
  analysis, setting up 182
  measurement 61–6
  reduced 151
  sourcing information 173
Countrywide Communications **57, 58**
coverage
  adverse 126;
    see also BNA
  advertising 167
  beneficial;
    see BNA
  client plus competitor 122
  comparing 40
  competitor 41
  corporate, and issue management 181–8
  country **89**, 179–80
  cuttings bureaux and 21
  disproportionate 122
  editorial 65, 70, 72
    enquiries as a result of **64,** *68, 159*
  features 224
  FMCG 146
  forecasting attitudes to 96–7
  full page exclusive 51
  high share of 64
  identifying, on the page 33–6
  impact of 79
  industry **39,** *40,* **101, 106, 108, 118**
    selected releases/products appearances **105**
    total client **121,** *123*
  key journals 227
  leading, by country **89**
  managing 113–15

measuring 28–40
mix of 155
niche 105
past, used in evidence 194
peaks 113, 115
  and troughs 105
performance 154
peripheral 123
photographic 185
politics and 175–80
predicting 120–1
press releases 219–22
prior media, research 166
publishing formulae and 125
reach of 128–30
share **63**, 68
superior 40
syndicated 19
target 172
target journal 204
tertiary 123
tracking 28–9, 98, 111–26, 168, 176, 181
understanding, for effectiveness 159–68
value of, in its market-place 143–4
Cranfield School of Management 14, 61
creativity 154, 168
Cresson, Édith **91**
cross-referencing 56
cultures 169, 170, 179, 180
cuttings 111, 136, 145, 182, 229
  absolute and proportional length 109
  analysis 86, 116, 144, 203
  archiving 31
  attribution and 78
  bureaux 20–2, 23–4, 192, 202
    inadequacy 198
    reliable 170
    response time **30**
  ccm and 40, 114
  checklist 31

client and competition *116*, **117**
entered for month published **32**
getting 19–20
incorrect 27
keeping in chronological order 30–1
management log of 26
matching to source 56–8
measurement technology and evaluation 160
measuring 29–31, 80
more important role for 192
number per category 228
previous, studies of 157
received by week and month **37**, *40*
records 26
relationship between ccm and 114
relevant 22
reliable source 29
sourcing 171
specification 27, 206–9
surrounding articles frequently excluded from 44

data 105, 115, 150, 153, 190
  corrupt or inaccessible 142
  electronic, absence/lack of 171, 199
  expenditure 184
  historic 135, 158
  investment 182
  market information 71
  mechanical 146
  quantifiable 196
  recall 142
  software 141
databanks 197
databases 58, 134–5, 136, 142, 145, 181
  deficiency 171
  electronic 181
  journals 172
  'off-the-shelf' software 141

on-line 20
relational 140
see also Press Relations Performance Review
Delors, Jacques 91
Denman, R **91**
Department of Trade and Industry 196
detraction 96, 97, 98
direct mail 20, 138
direct marketing 151, 195
discipline 189
discretion 96
distribution 53, 134
focused 41

Eastern Europe 89, 90, 200
EC (European Community) 88–92, 161, 198–9
  Commission 19
editorials 84, 145, 146, 172, 195
  analysis 169
  better knowledge of needs 191
  changing attitudes 125
  context 196
  coverage 65, 68, 70, 72
  enquiries and **64**, *159*
  decisions 59, 131
  headlines and photographs **46**, *47*
  impact 159–60
  power and 147
  magazine 78, 79
  mentions 66
  message 42–6
  national newspapers 175
  need assessment 150–1
  opinion-moulding 89
  PR-led 78, 79
  space 121, 162
  see also ESU
editors 84, 134, 189, 195
effectiveness
  articles 147–8
  assessing 107

Index

case studies 163, 166–7
consultancies 192
cost 184, 198
journals 195
measurement 184
messages 51, **53**, 177
monitoring 26–7, 56, 85, 175, 179
most elementary record of 112
PR 63, 184
press offices 29
understanding coverage for 159–68
elections 116, 178
electronic libraries 182, 197
enquiries **62**, 76, 77, 135, 163, 167
following share coverage **63**
high level 68
measuring 163–4
need to attract a lot 158
response tracking 119
result of editorial coverage **64, 68**, *159*
ESU (editorial space universe) 121–4, 135, 144, 155, 176, 190, 205
comparing 185
contracting 187
for issues 125
narrow 164
no way of knowing size of 166
share of 163, 182
tourist promotion and 180
Ethiopia 73
euphemism 100
evaluation 19, 21, 105
accurate 54
counting words 33
effect of, on the media 193
importance and content 22
multimedia 165
poor 41
response 76
rising popularity of 199
exclusions 207, 209
exclusivity 51, 105, 171, 211

Falklands war 73
features 224
feedback 189–90
financial commitment 132–4
financial institutions 182
Financial Times 187, 218, 227
foreign language 173
'fortress Europe' policy 89
France 169, 172
free sheets 21, 138
FT Profile 20, 35
future forecasting 125

Gallup 89, 91
GEC CEGELEC 42
generic names 23, 116
Germany 85, 89, 161, 172, 173
global service 87
Gonzales, F **91**
Grocer, The 218, 219, 227
Gulf War 69–70, 71, 80, 81, 98, 200

Hahn, C **91**
Haughey, Charles **91**
Hayes Macleod 85
headlines 36, 48, 71, 91, 171, 203
banner 33, 47
editorial and advertising **46**
eye-catching 42
'Gotcha' 73, 76
issues 125, 178
names in 51, 61, 109, 169, 204
off the page impact 35
Hellar, P **91**
Hills, Carla 90, **91**
historical analysis 104–7
Hollis Europe 173
Holtrop, Thomas 85, 86, 87

ideas 18, 162
identification 56, 59, 118
attitudes 85, 186
campaign needs 155
circulation 80
coverage on the page 33–6

faster 165
issues 96, 119
journalists 178, 180
politically famous 176-7
publications 41, 139, 155, 194-5
readership 80, 135
regional strengths or weakness 178
sources 109-10, 124, 186
success of competitors 40
unworthy publications 194-5
image 85, 86, 93, 98, 119
  brand 183
  client 59
  negative 87
  profile growth 126
impact 71, 123, 138, 145, 171, 191
  across the world 169
  advertising 68
  analysis, more precise 198
  assessing **50**, 53, 82
    trends in 119
  benign, on environmental issues 156
  campaign 151
    planning 107
  competition 152
  coverage 79
  editorial 147, 159-60
  high 162
  knowing which publications have greater 131
  measuring 41-54, 76, 190
    method for 33
    off the page 35, 51
    on the page **34**
    rating 48-51
  media 181, 195
  more precise analysis of 198
  predictions 155
  public attitudes 72
  public relations 192, 193
  radio and television 199
  reader 38, 64
  relative 47, 59

repetition 143
residual 163
small difference in 36
story on the page 98
values 36, 54, 124, 127
worthwhile 120
inaccuracy 96, 197
influence 68-70, 72, 79, 96, 97-8, 108
  chain of 130-1
  most important 84
  negative trends and 86
  photographs 35
information
  ability to track sources for 196
  about British publications 202
  adding 142
  advance 121
  attitude, behavioural change and 73-5
  available from comparative analysis 104
  available to journalists 194
  cost of sourcing 173
  electronic libraries of 197
  key 42
  market 71
  third-party sources 204
Ingersoll Rand 19
Institute of Public Relations 13, 14, 191
international law 173
international press programmes 169-74
interpretive skills 142, 154, 157
invitations 134-5
Iraq 69, 71, 80, 81, 98, 179, 187
issues 109, 121, 179, 186, 196
  assumed 190
  attitudes towards 102
  blurred 100
  brand specific 87
  closely related 103
  comparing 185
  competing 187
  competitors and 103

Index

complex 168
environmental 156
evolution and favourability 92
headline 178
identifying 96, 119
important 178
key 80, 84
leading sectoral **90**
likelihood of being eclipsed 120
local 139
major 125, 153
management 156, 184–5, 204
multiple 103–4
other 98
 focusing on 156–7
political 116, 139
popularity 176, 178
relevance of 125, 191
tracking, from coast to coast **88**
trends and 28–9
Italy 171

jargon 100, 202
journalists 56, 77–8, 87, 99, 185, 196
 attitudes 41, 84–5
 background material available to 197
 bylined 204
 effect of coverage analysis on 193
 highly targeted conversations to 151
 identifying 178, 180
 idle 187
 information available to 194
 key 70, 175
 knowing volume and nature of coverage 58
 list of contacts with 59
 names of 84, 226
 neutral material and 110
 relationship between press officers and 200
 specialist 109
 staff 172
 targeted 132, 134
 unexpected 178
journals 54, 84, 128–35, 158, 162
 computer-based agencies and 21
 covering client industry 123, **124**
 database of 172
 different 107, 115
 ethnic 180
 heavyweight 69
 identifying 41, 155
 industry coverage 65, *105*, **106**
 key 70, 109, 166, 203, 227
 monthly 36
 niche 22
 other 98, 157, 197
 peripheral 134, 157
 providing interest for 120
 range of 145
 rating of effectiveness 195
 readership 80, 157
 readers' perceptions of 101
 regularly published, in Britain 19
 relevance limited to effectiveness 78
 relevant 41, 127, 136
 same, repetition of story 143
 selected 61, **106**, 128, **129**, *130*
 specialist 164
 successful 125
 target coverage 203, 204
 technical 71
 trade 167
 typical record of, covering a client *132*, **133**
 wide spectrum 182
judgements 120, 121, 144
 long-term 119
 qualitative 99, 113
key words 21, 22, 23–4, 58, 78, 92
 additional 209
 BNA applied to 83, 97
 direct attribution 93, 205
 hierarchy 82
 in context 44, **45**
 journalists' names and 84
 mentions 36

multi 209
occurrences 174
other notable 81-2, 203
principal 80, 82, 202-3, 209
repeated 96
secondary 82, 203
single 206-8
knowledge gap 165-8, 190
Kohl, Helmut 90, **91**
Kuwait 72, 187

labelling 56, 57
Lambsdorff, O **91**
language 100, 169, 173
'language of success' 54
layout 146
letters column 84-5
lifestyle 70
Lindenmann, Walter 19
local media/press 54, 135, 178, 228
 newspapers 128, 180
 publications 136, 138, 139, 146
 radio and television 137
Lyng, R **91**

Maastricht 161
McGraw Hill **91**
McLeod, Jack 19
Macleod, Sandra 85
Mclure, Robert D 19
magazines 167, 172, 180
 competing 134
 computer 29, 160
 diet 71
 mass-market 71
 peripheral 123
 popular-science 71
 slimming and health 79
 specialist 70
 women's 78-9
Manager Magazine 85
market leadership 167
market research 76, 168
market share 62, 63, 149
marketing 105, 155

direct 151, 195
niche 52, 131
tactical 138
Maxwell, Robert 70
meaning 100
measurement 58, 83, 105, 149, 156, 165
 acceptance and 96, 97, 98
 agencies 199
 attitudes to plan campaigns 99
 common 171
 constant 95, 186-7
 consumer trends 160-2
 coverage 28-40
 effect of editorial on behaviour 75-6
 enquiries 163-4
 historic 125
 impact 41-54, 76, 190
 column centimetres and area 48, **49**
 method for 33
 off the page 35, 51
 on the page **34**
 rating 48-51
 methodology 140-2
 more complicated 47-8
 nominal 147
 off-the-page response 76
 one system of 144
 press cuttings 29-31
 principles of 104
 quantitative/qualitative 80
 recent developments in technology 160
 regional campaign 135-8
 relative 106
 space 35
 spurious 44
media 18, 54, 189-97
 attitudes 180
 buying 127-8, 132
 change in opinion 156
 effect of evaluation on 193
 electronic 19, 20

Index

enhanced selection 190
exposure 28–9
future campaigns 125
image 181, 195
impact 195
influence 70
less reliable 124
lists 56, 58, 150
manipulation 77
and the market 28, **29**
monitoring 182, 183
national 175
pervasiveness across 151
right 54
specialist 28, 71, 183
tracking methods 197
written 164
see also local media
Media Measurement Limited 63, 71, 161
see also Press Relations Performance Review
mentions 59, 163, 172
  editorial 66
  key word 36
  unsolicited 63
  unusual 27
Merriam, John E 19, 28, 71, 160
messages
  ability to progress 167
  achieved through advertising 115
  conveyed 229
  delivery 143
    method of assessing effectiveness in core publications 51, **53**
    potential, identifying **137**
  editorial 42–6, 75
  effectiveness of, and regional targeting 177
  focused 68
  how interpreted 96
  key 89
  shaping 150

written media an effective carrier 164
Middle East 80, 81, 83, 109
Mirror Group 70
misinterpretation 173
Mitterrand, François 90, **91**
monitoring 100, 109, 156, 167, 186, 193
  advanced 84
  as advertising 143–8
  brand image 183
  careful 168
  content 61
  context, used for advertising policy 195–6
  corporate identity 184
  effective **57**
  effectiveness 85, 175, 179
    and follow up 26–7
  historic publishing practices 134
  important area for 165
  improved 194
  media 183
    covering investment news 182
  one of the key uses for monitoring 184
  'opportunities to read' 128
  other issues 98
  output 55–66
  peaks and troughs 116
  specific attitudes 180
  trials 174
  variance 115
  see also ESU
Mosbacher, R **91**
motivation 69, 76, 159, 165, 191
  behind behavioural change 73, 75
Naisbitt, John 19
names
  associated 207, 209
  brand 79, 183, 207
  generic 23, 116
  in headlines 51, 61, 109, 169
    and photographs 204
  journalists' 84, 226

National Media Index 28
Nazi press 18
neutral rating, *see* BNA
Newman, Warren 143
news 121, 122
   environmental 160
   front-page 44, 125
   investment 182–3
   neutral 73
newsletters 48, 71
newspapers 19, 29, 102, 169, 172, 182
   circulation 137, 160
   daily 71, 185
   evening 137–8
   local 128, 180
   major 180
   national 48, 78, 175, 178, 183, 185
   serious 164
   popular 136, 172, 195
   weekly 136
niche marketing 52, 131
North Africa 73
numeracy 191

one-on-one letters and memos 20
opinion 89, 96, 156, 196, 200
   forming 72, 123, 131
      tertiary 200
   influenced 69
   informed 201
   shaping/cultivating 70, 177
opinion formers 85, 87, 103, 152, 179
opinion polls 18, 92, 95, 163
'opportunities to read' **130**, 190, 204
output *111*, **112**, 113, 186, 219–22, 225–6
   monitoring 55–66

page positions 44, **45**, 146
Panorama 196
Parliament 69
peaks 113, 115, 161

and troughs *105*, 121–2
peer pressure 68
penetration
   in articles **142**
   household 96, 137, 146–7
   market 163
   specialist 151
   tracking 138
perceptions 89, 101
   audience 82, 92–3, 95, 97, 100
performance 99, 100, 154, 156, 190
   bonuses 155
   campaign 173
   monitoring 156
   poor 119
   press relations 152–3, 169–71
   relative 102
   specifying criteria 153
   statistical measurement of 140
   targets 149
   versus cost 154
periodicals 19, 20
pervasiveness 151, 181, 182
photographs 33, *36*, 54, 104, 105, 109, 135, 146, 153, 158, 171, 185, 194, 203, 231
   caption to 23
   and changing national attitudes 73
   impact across the world 169
   name in headline and 51, 204
   presence and influence 35
   striking/poor 47
phrases 58, 80, 81, 96, 202
plagiarism monitor 196
planning 104, 138, 141
   campaign 53, 84, 99, 127–8, 140, 149–58
   future 95, 125
   impact on 107
   forward, of advertisements 146
   future long-term 109
   resource 152
   strategic and tactical 116
   using ESU 123

Index

Poland 180
politics 69, 175–80
polling organisations, *see* opinion polls
postcodes 136–7, 146
PR (public relations) 64, 72, 97, 120, 157, 164
 and behavioural change 95
 campaigns 83, 93
 editorials 78, 79
 effectiveness *63*, 184
 impact 192, 193
 journalists and 77
 low level of commitment to 117
 more professionalism from press and 193–4
 practitioners 35, 172, 199, 200
 consultants 121, 131
 in-house teams 86
 managers 87, 119, 130, 154, 158
 press relations as component of 155–6
 resources allocation for 85, 105
 role 73
 see also Institute of Public Relations
prediction 75, 124, 156
 coverage 120–1
 peaks and troughs 122
 public attitudes and opinions 92
 quality of 125, 165
 share values 182–3
press lists 55–6, 132, 136, 204
 normal 168
 provisional 157
press officers 41
 good 55, 194
 numerate press 191
 relationship between journalists and 201
 relative strength 107–9
press relations
 analysis for the marketeer 120
 campaigns 54, 76, 140, 165, 173
 choice of 152
 component of PR 155–6
 essential basic skills for 154
 expenditure 184
 performance-related 120, 152–3, 169–71
 Press Relations Performance Review 202, 203, 204
 press releases 57, 63, 113, 152, 158, 184
 assignment of 59
 average articles **38**
 blanket approach to issuing 66
 cost of sourcing for 173
 coverage 223
 existing stocks 111
 issuing like confetti 134
 looking forward to receiving 193
 output 104, *111*, **112**, 219–22
 quality of 42
 type and 115
 referencing 56
 rewriting 44
 translated 173
 writers 194
products **105**
 associated names and 207, 209
 competitors' 167
 development 156
 launches 115, 134, 150, 157, 166
 management 154
 measurements 109
 press relations 155
 promoting into wider markets 166
 USP of 109, 162
professionalism 193–4, 200
 lack of 85
profile 116–19, 177
 image 126
 local 156
 readership 44, 137
promotional activities 106, 138, 154, 166, 183, 198
 benefit 109–10
 campaigns 105

245

propositions 96, 97, 98–9, 162, 170, 190
provincial press, *see* local media
public opinion 69, 70, 85, 200
Public Relations Consultants Association 61
publications
 analysis 59, **60**
 anticipated 26, 207
 British, information about 202
 core 22, *51*, **53**
 different, number of 96
 hierarchy of 130
 highbrow 164
 identifying 139, 194–5
 important 54, 153
 influenced by other factors 108
 influential 70
 key 175, 203
 knowing which have greater impact 131
 limited number of 42
 local 136, 138, 139, 146
 main line target 124
 maintaining records 132, 150
 monthly 138
 most effective mix of stories and 153–4
 most essential types 158
 most frequent 204
 national 135
 obvious target 167
 other 137, 185
 particular 107
 peripheral 124
 reader's regard for the content 101
 refined lists 127
 relative value of 145
 relevant 19, 38
 sampling 160
 sheer numbers of 195
 space devoted to subject in 39
 specialist 69, 169
 specific types 20
 specifying, for a press list 136
 successful 44
 target 130
 technical 47
 tertiary 123–4
 tracking 131
 trade 47, 128, 168
 unworthy 194–5
 wider-circulation 71
 see also free sheets; journals; magazines; newsletters; newspapers; periodicals
publicity 131, 138, 163

quantitative/qualitative measures 80

radio 19, 54, 69
 local 137
ratings 76, 102
 prominence 95
 see also BNA
reach **129**, 135, 136, 146–7, 185
 circulation 130, 161, 164
 regional 90
 relevance and 22
readers 71, 79–80, 96
 attempt to fool 172
 attention 44
 great influence on 68
 impact measurement and 48
 impact on 38, 64
 motivations 191
 perceptions of journals 101
 regard for the content of a publication 101
 stimulation for 70, 76
 subliminal effect on 42
 understanding of language 100
readership 22, 78, 136, 200
 and content 35
 estimates 128
 identification 80
 by socioeconomic group 135
 journal 80, 157
 levels of acceptance between

Index

35–6
  most appropriate 127
  motivation for 165
  new 131
  particular 125
  profile 44, 137
  relevant 33
  wider 162
Reagan, Ronald **91**
records 115, *132*, **133**, 134, 150, 154
  cuttings 29–30
  see also databases
references 56, 173
Regional Media Centre 136
regional press 136, 178
reporters, *see* journalists
reports *107*, **108**
  detailed 204–5
  errors 196
  frequency 36–40
  neutral 110
  progressive 109
  written 203
research 61, 102, 145, 164
  'akin' 163
  audience 59, 100
  based on impact of coverage 35
  broader 159
  desk 197
  detailed 77, 170
  future campaign planning 95
  independent, for perceptions 95
  local lists 135
  market 76, 168
  media buying 132
  need for 76–7
  opinion 179
  post campaign 143
  prior media coverage 166
  simple and easily executed 156
  violence on television 199
  see also analysis; CARMA; content analysis; databases
resource monitor 107
response 28, 76, 160, 161, 185
  highest generation 152
  optimum 154
  press-prompted 67–77
  sales enquiry tracking 119
Ricoh Co **91**
Romeike and Curtice 23, 58, 203
Rothmans 19
Ruggiero, R **91**
Russia 169, 180

Saddam Hussein 69, 82, 83, 94
safety 99
scanners 33
Schwarzkopf, General 80, 81
share prices 125
Shaw, Donald L 19
silly season 187
slang 100
Social Charter 90
software 58, 140–1, 146
Sony 92
sound bites 169
sources 58, 89, 180
  ability to track, for information 196
  analysis 177
  competing 78
  external, contributions from 84
  favourable **91**
  identification 109–10, 124, 186
  leading *90*, **91**
  matching cuttings to 56–8
  material 102
  most reported 204
  news 90
  reliable, for press cuttings 29
  stories 152
  third-party 204
  unfavourable **90**
sourcing
  cost of 173
  cuttings 171
  news 20
Soviet Union 180
space 35, 39, 48, 120

advertising 146
editorial 42, 121, 162;
  see also ESU
value 65, 147
Spain 86, 87
specialist organisations 20
specialist press 164-5
'spikes' 122-3
spokespersons 58, 81, 83, 109, 152
  key 177
  selected 124
statistics 62, 115, 190, 191, 196
  analysis 176
  measurement of performance 140
stories 59, 115, 138, 164
  different, acceptability of 105-7
  life of 71, 105
  most effective mix of
    publications and 153-4
  negative 88
  similar 134
  simple 167
  sources of 152
  specific 104
  spread 139
style 61, 79, 138
  and content 59-61, 73, 75, 104,
    191, 194
  difference in 172-3
subcontractor/consultancy
  agreement 210-17
subjects/subject matter 79, 124,
  155, 187
  interest in 120, 194
  space devoted to 39
  selected 21
subsidiaries 170, 183-4
Sun 35, 73, **74**
Super Marketing 227

targeting 42, 58, 127-39
  behavioural change 95
  close 195
  effective 54
  value of 52-3

targets **137**, 153, 155
  attainment 170
  audiences 137, 167
  readership 35
  setting 151-2
telephone interviews 89
television 19, 54, 69, 70, 90, 196
  impact 199
  local 137
  more believable than
    newspapers 102
  prime-time 131
  violence on 164, 199
tertiary words 81-2, 83
Thatcher, Margaret 90, **91**
Times 145
timing 44, 115-16, 124
  importance of 44, **45**
tourism 180
tracking 59, 61, 68, 153-4, 160,
  194-5, 198
  ability 196
  all interested publications 131
  attitudinal change 84, 98
  back 115
  capability 204
  case studies 115, 117-18
  changes in market 86
  charting and 141
  competitors 104
  content analysis and 18
  coverage 28-9, 98, 111-26, 168,
    176, 181
  date 135
  effective 187
  future 95
  important to maintain 110
  issues 103, 177, 197
    coast to coast **88**
  media-, methods 197
  penetration 138
  political issues 139
  pressure groups 177
  profile, industrial applications
    for 116-19

Index

record over a number of
   campaigns 115
records 157
resource allocation and 119–20
sales enquiry response 119
share of voice 186
sources 186
studies 71
worldwide 20
trade associations 180
trade papers 20
trends 19, 37, 38, 90, 116, 186
   consumer, measuring 160–2
   impact assessment 119
   issues and 28–9
   national, variance with 177
   negative 86
   regional market 138
   social and economic 18
trials 174

United States 71, 116, 179, 180, 182, 199
   attitudes to the European Single Market **88**
   city watch 125–6
   content analysis 18–19
   detailed analysis 198
   ESU 176
   public relations practice 169
   tracking 28, 130, 160,
   see also American Express; Gulf War

vacuum cleaners 23
validation 76
value for money 87
values 75, 80, 165
   ascribing, to measures of press articles *51*, **52**
   impact 36, 54, 124, 127
   nominal 147
   share 182–3
variables 96, 145–6
variance/variation 114–15, 119, 177
   predictable 122
visibility cycles 113
voting behaviour 73–5

Wall Street Journal 35, 145
war 69, 83
Washington Post 70
wastage level 131
wasted effort 151
'watch-dog' organisations 181
Watergate 70
Weaver, David H 18–19
Welbeck Golin/Harris study 78, 79, 128
White House 81, 83
word counts 33–5, 81
word processing packages 140–1

yesterday's news 71
Yeulter, C **91**
Yorkshire Post 137